# Reporting to Court
## Under the Children Act

**A Handbook for Social Services**

Penny Cooper

information & publishing solutions

Published by TSO (The Stationery Office) and available from:

**Online**
**www.tsoshop.co.uk**

**Mail, Telephone, Fax & E-mail**
TSO
PO Box 29, Norwich, NR3 1GN
Telephone orders/General enquiries: 0870 600 5522
Fax orders: 0870 600 5533
E-mail: customer.services@tso.co.uk
Textphone: 0870 240 3701

**TSO@Blackwell and other Accredited Agents**

**Customers can also order publications from:**
TSO Ireland
16 Arthur Street, Belfast BT1 4GD
Tel 028 9023 8451    Fax 028 9023 5401

First published 1996

Second edition 2006

Third impression 2010

ISBN: 978 0 11 271189 6

Printed in the United Kingdom for The Stationery Office
ID 5404992   C1   5375   19585

# Reporting to Court
## Under the Children Act

**A Handbook for Social Services**

Penny Cooper

London: TSO

# About the Author

Penny Cooper is a barrister and training consultant. She is an Associate Dean at the Inns of Court School of Law and Director of Knowledge Transfer at The City Law School, City University, London.

Penny designs and delivers tailor-made, participative training for professionals. She has specialised for many years in witness familiarisation and report writing. Penny also leads the Registered Intermediary legal training scheme for the Office for Criminal Justice Reform. Intermediaries are part of "special measures"; they assist in communication with vulnerable witnesses. Penny was recognised by the DfES for her contribution to their Information Sharing Training consultation.

Penny graduated with a joint honours degree from Leicester Polytechnic in 1989 and studied for the Bar at The Inns of Court School of Law. She then practised as a barrister from 3 Paper Buildings, London. She spent almost six years providing in-house legal advice to the London Boroughs of Wandsworth and Hammersmith and Fulham before returning to private practice where she was instructed by many local authorities in London and the South East.

In addition to her full-time work at City University, Penny is an elected District Councillor. She is the Member for Children and Young People on her local Council.

**Penny Cooper**
**E-mail: reportingtocourt@aol.com**

# Preface 2006

The decision to update the excellent 1st Edition of 'Reporting to Court' is to be applauded. Reference to the progress towards yet better practice, which is reflected in case law and, most significantly, in the 'The Protocol' on delay and the 2006 Review of Child Care Proceedings has been interwoven with the previous text. The result is an up to date handbook which gives sound, practical guidance to practitioners at all levels of the social services network who are required to contribute to the Family Court process. The necessary detail is explained in plain language and is supported by flowcharts and diagrams; the result continues to be a very accessible document.

When in practice at the Bar, I more than once used 'Reporting to Court' to cross examine hapless social workers who had failed to follow its terms. This new edition should be required reading for all practitioners. Those who follow its advice will not only be 'bomb-proof' against such questioning but, more importantly, will have presented the results of their work to the court in the most effective manner.

**The Hon. Mr Justice McFarlane**

# Acknowledgements 2006

Firstly my thanks go to the original authors, Joyce Plotnikoff and Richard Woolfson of Lexicon Limited. I met Joyce and Richard through our involvement in the Registered Intermediary training scheme. It was Joyce who suggested that I might like to update Reporting to Court. I was very honoured because this little blue book that was first published in 1996 has become a social work classic, much referred to and often quoted. Joyce and Richard are highly regarded for their ongoing contributions to the law relating to children and to criminal justice reform. I only hope that this edition lives up to their very high standard.

I would like to express my heartfelt thanks to my advisory group for their comments and advice on this new version of the handbook. Your experience and knowledge were invaluable.

Thank you:

Peter Greene, District Judge of the Principal Registry of the Family Division,
Geraldine Howard,
Courtney Plank,
Carol Platteuw,
Joanne Ross and
Annette Warrick.

My thanks go to all my team at the Inns of Court School of Law, CPD Department, but in particular Catherine Groch and David Wurtzel. I am also grateful to Adam Scott and Corinne Barker of TSO and Kevin Beale of the Legal Department and Bernadette Boland of the Child Protection Training Team at the London Borough of Hammersmith and Fulham.

Last but definitely not least I thank my husband Bob and our boys, Christopher and Bobby. I hope that each of you knows just how much your support means to me. Christopher and Bobby, your lovely drawings of flowers and a computer now adorn the front cover and inside pages of this new edition of Reporting to Court.

**Penny Cooper, June 2006**

# Preface 1996

I was delighted to be asked to write this Preface because of what I believe to be the importance of the work that follows it. My real qualification for doing so is experience based on the thousands of pages of reports which I must have read in twenty years' practice in the field of child care as a barrister and latterly as a Circuit Judge.

Over the last few years there has been a significant change in the practice of the civil courts. The traditional dependence on oral evidence has been replaced by an increasing emphasis on setting out cases in writing with consequent curbs on such evidence. Alongside that has gone a new level of scrutiny of local authority plans and the giving of much greater importance to the maintenance of contact between children and their natural families. All this requires early and careful thought by social work practitioners.

Giving evidence or writing a report for court is a specialist skill that is not acquired merely through general social work experience. These reports are not primarily for fellow child care professionals but for magistrates, judges, advocates and their clients. They require both care and proper time for preparation. Courts pre-read reports and the cogent, succinct and obviously well thought out report is not only a great asset but also inspires confidence in the writer. It is always sad when a long, rambling report has the effect of not just concealing but actually undermining what was in fact sound professional practice on the ground.

Hence my warm welcome for this Handbook. The Department of Health has done a signal service in initiating this project and the consultants have provided what I believe will prove a resource of high quality and practical usefulness. The skill and knowledge of the Reference Group, together with others who have kindly assisted, has ensured rigorous scrutiny of the material. Moreover, it has been tried in practice and revised in the light of experience.

This is a Handbook for daily use, not an impressive volume for a bookcase decoration. It is written with the needs of the busy (and even nervous) practitioner in mind. Its style and layout makes it easy to use and its scope is sufficient for all practical purposes. I commend it enthusiastically to all social workers who share in the vital work of promoting the welfare of children through the civil justice system.

**His Honour Judge Mark Hedley**

# Acknowledgements 1996

Many people gave freely of their time and experience during the production of the Handbook. Special thanks are due to Wendy Rose, Assistant Chief Inspector, who had overall responsibility for the project and to Arran Poyser, Social Services Inspector, for

shepherding the project to completion and chairing the project's Reference Group. Its members included:

Chris Bazell, Clerk to the Justices, Banbury and Bicester Magistrates' Courts
Keith Bilton, Chair, Children and Families Subcommittee, British Association of Social Workers
Clare Bridges, Deputy Clerk to the Justices, Croydon Magistrates' Court
Collette Curran, Social worker/ therapist, NSPCC
Rose Dagoo, guardian ad litem and social work consultant
Ann Haig, project leader, Barnardos Counselling Services and guardian ad litem
Ann Mair, Chair, Family Proceedings Committee, Magistrates' Association
Caroline Rowe, Probation Service Division, Home Office
Annie Shepperd, Assistant Director, Children and Families, Sutton Social Services Department
Philip Thomson, Head of Legal Services, Essex County Council
Myra White, Civil and Family Business Branch, Court Service
Trish White, Social Services Inspector, Welsh Office.

Mr Justice Wall and His Honour Judge Hedley provided comments on the draft and Judge Hedley kindly agreed to write the Preface to the Handbook.

Southwark Council participated in a four month field test of the draft Handbook which resulted in substantial revisions. We are indebted to Anne Chan, Assistant Director, Children's Services and Gloria McFarlane, Acting Head of Legal Services for their cooperation, and to all the members of their staff who provided constructive criticism. Feedback was also provided by lawyers and others in the court process who read Social Services' statements which had been written with reference to the Handbook. The evaluation was facilitated by Elizabeth Thompson, senior chief clerk, Inner London Family Proceedings Courts; Ruth Ewen, principal clerk, Children Branch, Principal Registry Family Division; and Anna Faulkner, panel manager, Inner and North London Panel of Guardians ad Litem.

Legal citations were checked by Nicola Harrington, Legal Services Division, Essex County Council. Advice on other aspects of the Handbook was provided by:

Jeremy Barley, solicitor, Ronald Prior and Co. Walthamstow, London (Association of Lawyers for Children)
Sarah Borthwick, trainer consultant, British Agencies for Adoption and Fostering
Graham Cole, senior solicitor, Bedfordshire Legal Services
Jacqueline Drennan, foster carer, Bedfordshire

Janice Edgington, assistant lawyer, Legal Services, Lewisham Legal Services

Philippa Evans, senior principal solicitor, Coventry (Law Society Child Care Law Joint Liaison Group)

Fiona Ledden, assistant solicitor, Sutton Legal Services (Association of Lawyers for Children)

Ann Molloy, principal solicitor, Child Care Business Unit, Liverpool Legal Services (Law Society Child Care Law Joint Liaison Group)

Geoff Orton, National Foster Care Association

Alberta Owusu, principal solicitor, Barnet Legal Services

Peter Riches, Director, LBTC: Training For Care

Paddy Sheehy, guardian ad litem

Ann Stevens, assistant solicitor, Sutton Legal Services

Geoff Wild, solicitor, Kent Legal Services

Val Wykes, Children and Families Team, Westminster Social Services Department.

In the Department of Health, thanks are due to Jim Brown for his indispensable administrative support, and to Marianne Harper for help with the design and publication.

We would like to acknowledge our debt to the following primary sources which we found both thorough and accessible:

Adcock M., White R. and Hollows A. Significant Harm: its management and outcome (1991) Significant Publications.

Brayne H. and Martin G. Law for Social Workers (1990) Blackstone Press Ltd. 3rd edition.

National Standards for Probation Service Family Court Work (1994) Home Office.

Pizzey S. and Davis S. A Guide for Guardians ad Litem in Public Law Proceedings under the Children Act 1989 (1995) HMSO.

Ryan M. The Children Act 1989 - Putting it into Practice (1994) Family Rights Group, Arena.

Timms J. Children's Representation - a practitioner's guide (1995) Sweet and Maxwell.

Illustrations were provided by children from Craigholme School and Hutchesons' School, Glasgow and Preston Primary School, Hertfordshire.

# Contents

Preface v

Acknowledgements vi

1 Introduction 1

2 Preparation 6

3 Timetabling at court and within the local authority 11

4 The local authority legal adviser 17

5 Working with experts and other key participants 20

6 Public law applications 27

7 Private law: court-ordered enquiries 38

8 Content and layout 45

9 Starting the document 52

10 The parents 56

| 11 | The child | 58 |
| 12 | The local authority plan for contact | 62 |
| 13 | The local authority plan for care of the child | 69 |
| 14 | Coming to a conclusion | 75 |
| 15 | Giving evidence at court | 78 |
| | Annexes One to Six | 82 |

# List of figures

Figure 1:  Guiding principles in the Children Act                                              4

Figure 2:  Court structure for proceedings under the Children Act 1989           18

Figure 3:  Children Act orders giving authority for temporary removal of a child   30

Figure 4:  Significant harm criteria                                                         33

Figure 5:  Selecting what should go into your statement                             51

# Introduction

This Handbook aims to help you improve the quality of your written submissions in Children Act proceedings.

## Why strive for high standards in reporting to court?

- to promote the best interests of the child
- to provide accurate, accessible and relevant information
- to provide a sound foundation for the action being requested from the court
- because well structured and clearly presented written material is the best preparation for giving oral evidence
- because all written material submitted to the court is automatically disclosed to all the parties before a hearing.

This chapter tells you about the scope of the Handbook and how to use it.

## Who is the Handbook for?

The guidance is primarily intended for use within the social services network, for example by:

- practitioners working directly with children and their families
- those managing and supervising this work
- service providers involved in the development of care plans
- family centre staff
- residential workers
- trainers
- and legal advisers to child and family professionals.

Parts of the Handbook should also prove useful to foster carers and professionals in health and education when preparing their statements for court.

The Handbook is not intended to replace advice from the local authority legal adviser.

## What does the Handbook cover?

The Handbook relates to public and private law applications under the Children Act 1989. Care proceedings are an example of public law regulating the intervention of the local authority in parental care of children. Divorce proceedings are an example of private law covering disputes between individuals.

The Handbook does not cover adoption proceedings, the Human Fertilisation and Embryology

Act 1990[1], criminal proceedings[2], or reports prepared by children's guardians (guardians)[3] or probation officers[4].

## Public law statements and private law reports

When you provide a statement in public law proceedings, it contains evidence that the local authority intends to put before the court . 'Evidence' is any material placed before the court to persuade it of the truth or probability of some fact. Unless the other parties accept what you have put in your statement, you can expect to be cross-examined on your statement. When you submit a report in a private law matter, the facts contained in the report may be treated as evidence and you may be cross-examined on them.

When the Children Act 1989 came into force in 1991, it required us to develop new approaches to written submissions to the court. Witness statements have been described as a sensible innovation aimed at a "cards on the table" approach[5]. Family proceedings are often described as non-adversarial because the court's paramount concern is the welfare of the child. Despite this non- adversarial approach you can expect to be rigorously tested on your statement. A carefully written statement will assist you when you come to give evidence particularly if it clearly identifies the facts upon which you base your conclusions.

However, preparation and writing are difficult activities, particularly when they are conducted under pressure of time and competing work demands.

## The court perspective

The court will welcome statements which help it to determine findings of fact and reasons for its decisions. In its inquisitorial role the court may ask questions which probe the issues and test the evidence. These tasks are made more difficult if judges have to sift through lengthy statements and reports in order to identify what is relevant. In some cases, they have described documents as:

- insufficiently focused
- failing to distinguish between fact and opinion
- reproducing large parts of case records with little editing or structure
- failing to discuss the best interests of the child.

## Coordinate local authority statements

Local authority statements in the same case are often repetitious. This can be avoided by consultation between authors and the legal adviser/s.

## Written material is disclosed to all parties

The Children Act places an emphasis on the disclosure of written submissions before a case is heard. To give everyone the chance to prepare their case and to ensure that the parties are on an equal footing, all parties are required to file witness statements from persons whose evidence they intend to call. These statements need to contain the substance of the oral evidence that the party intends to put before the court. Reports are disclosed in the same way.

## Include all relevant facts, not only those that support your case

When preparing a statement, you are expected to take an accurate and balanced view of the local authority case. You must expose all relevant facts to examination, whether or not they support the local authority's application, and set out the reasons for the order(s) applied for by the local authority.

It is sometimes difficult to identify what may be relevant to other parties; when in doubt, always consult your legal adviser.

Local authorities have a very high degree of responsibility for disclosure, and have been criticised by courts for omitting relevant information from statements. The local authority cannot omit something just because it may be prejudicial to its own performance or to the outcome it is seeking.

## How is the Handbook organised?

To help you structure the task of drafting statements and reports for the court, this Handbook offers:

- step-by-step advice
- examples
- checklists.

Materials in the Handbook should be adapted to your needs and experience as well as to local requirements.

The Handbook provides suggestions for good practice, not a prescription for the 'definitive' statement or report.

Equally, the checklists are not exhaustive and you may wish to add your own notes. Where there are specific requirements for what must be included in your statement, this is made clear in the text.

The Handbook breaks down the drafting of written evidence into its component parts. The chapters following this introduction are grouped into five categories

- chapters two to five assist in preparation, timetabling and liaison with others in the court process
- chapters six and seven describe the requirements of specific public and private law applications

- chapters eight to eleven address the content of your statement or report
- chapters twelve to fourteen cover the local authority's contact and care plans
- chapter fifteen contains guidance on giving evidence at court.

Throughout the Handbook, the term 'case conference' includes, where appropriate, child protection conferences.

The six Annexes include a checklist to assist foster carers in planning the content of their statements prior to discussion with the local authority legal adviser as well as a extracts from good practice guidance, a checklist for statement writing, tips for giving evidence at court, useful web site addresses and a brief description of the Human Rights Act 1998 and its implications.

Summaries of Children Act sections have been included in the text. When writing reports or statements, always check the Act itself and subsequent amendments. Discuss questions of interpretation with your local authority legal adviser. Case law cited in the Handbook is current as of May 2006.

**Figure 1: Guiding principles in the Children Act**

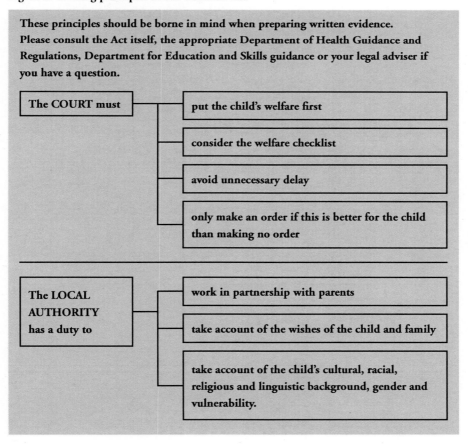

These principles should be borne in mind when preparing written evidence.
Please consult the Act itself, the appropriate Department of Health Guidance and Regulations, Department for Education and Skills guidance or your legal adviser if you have a question.

The COURT must
- put the child's welfare first
- consider the welfare checklist
- avoid unnecessary delay
- only make an order if this is better for the child than making no order

The LOCAL AUTHORITY has a duty to
- work in partnership with parents
- take account of the wishes of the child and family
- take account of the child's cultural, racial, religious and linguistic background, gender and vulnerability.

1  For the Human Fertilisation and Embryology Authority Code of Practice, see www.hfea.gov.uk

2  For pre-sentence reports, see www.nacro.org.uk for National Association for the Care and Resettlement of Offenders publications and advice.

3  Timms J. (1991) Manual of Practice for Guardians ad Litem and Reporting Officers. HMSO; Pizzey S. and Davis J. (1995) A Guide for Guardians ad Litem in Public Law Proceedings under the Children Act 1989. HMSO.

4  For national standards for probation practitioners, see www.probation.homeoffice.gov.uk

5  The Right Honourable the Lord Woolf (1995). Access to Justice: Interim report to the Lord Chancellor on the civil justice in England and Wales, section 3.9.

Reading the files Gillian (14)

# Preparation

**2**

You are more likely to produce a well-organised and focused statement for court
if you spend some time organising your thoughts and the materials first. The early
development of a chronology is vital and ideally should have been commenced as soon
as the file was opened. If there is not yet a chronology, now is the time to start one.
This chapter also suggests some other ideas to assist in preparation.

## The chronology

Every social work case file should have an up-to-date chronology at the front of the file so that
the allocated social worker or his or her manager can see the key events in the child's history. An
accurate, up-to-date chronology is one of the key tools that help a social worker and the court
assess the risks to a child.  A chronology should be started as soon as the file is opened in the
office. It should then be kept up to date by the allocated social worker adding new dates and
details as key events occur.

In any event, a social work chronology must be ready when an application is filed with the court.
The initial social work statement must also have been completed. These two vital documents
must be with the court within 2 days of the local authority application being issued at court.
This 2-day rule is set out in a document called the Protocol for Judicial Case Management in
Public Law Children Act Cases ("the Protocol"). Chapter 3 of this Handbook contains more
information on the steps in the Protocol and Annexe Two sets out key extracts from the Protocol.
The Protocol came into force on 1st November 2003 and all parties are expected to comply with
the guidance set out in it. It is sometimes called the "Protocol on Delay" since it aims reduce
delay in public law Children Act cases. Although not stated in the Protocol, it is the practice of
some courts not to accept an application without an initial social work statement and social work
chronology. In other words, your statement and chronology must already be complete when you
make an application for a care or supervision order.

The chronology will contain vital information for the court; it provides the court with a diary of
key dates and events in the child's life and could well be the first document that the court reads
before your application. The chronology should be prepared by the social worker not the legal
adviser. The chronology should be unbiased and factual.

The chronology acts:

* as an introduction to the case for the bench at the first hearing

* as a reference when drafting local authority statements

* to assist the guardian's enquiries.

If will often be necessary to file an updated chronology prior to the final hearing. Your legal
adviser should tell you when you need to prepare an updated chronology for the court.

The chronology provides a list of dates and key events which led up to the proceedings. It brings together factual information from the child protection register as well as from social work, medical and educational sources. It should:

- be succinct
- clearly identify key facts which can be agreed by all parties
- contain no opinion or judgement
- be clearly marked with the social services case reference number
- cross-reference other evidence or the documents on the social work file.

Events to be included in the chronology will depend on the circumstances of the case but may include:

- family history including marriages, births, deaths and changes in the make-up of the household
- the child's changes of address and school
- dates of case conferences and child protection registration
- key planning meetings
- relevant medical examinations
- incidents giving rise to concern
- child protection investigations
- history of children being accommodated voluntarily
- history of court applications, hearings and orders.

Example of part of a chronology:

| | | File Reference Number: XXXX |
|---|---|---|
| Date of Event | Description of Event | Source/Document on file |
| 29 October 2004 | Ms Vera Wilson left Rosie (then aged 4 months) in the care of her neighbours the Rowland family. After two days, Mrs Rowland called the emergency duty team. Rosie was accommodated voluntarily with foster parents Mr and Mrs Ellis. | Emergency duty role dated 31 October 2004, Social Work File 1 |
| 26 November 2004 | Mrs Ellis had to go into hospital so Rosie was moved to foster parent Mrs Drummond. | Officer's note File 1 |

| | | |
|---|---|---|
| 10 January 2004 | Ms Wilson removed Rosie from Mrs Drummond's care. They went to live in a hostel for the homeless. | |
| 15 April 2004 | At the request of her maternal grandmother Mrs Anne Wilson, who has taken care of Rosie overnight, Rosie was accommodated with foster parents Mr and Mrs Harris for five days. | Letter from Mrs Anne Wilson, File 1 |
| 16-18 May 2004 | Rosie was accommodated for two days at her mother's request with foster mother Mrs Newlands; Ms Wilson did not collect her. | Officer's note, File 2 |
| 18 May 2004 | Emergency Protection Order application; order made by the family proceedings court. | Copy E.P.O. File 2 |

Once you have compiled the up-to-date chronology you will be in a position to start thinking about preparing your statement.

## Identify key issues

The court does not know the background to your case. What is the purpose of the local authority application? Suppose you have to explain this orally. Take a few minutes to jot down the key issues, for example:

- what has happened?
- why is an order needed and what would be its purpose?
- why now?
- is an expert assessment needed (see chapter five)?

## Read the records

Some of the events that led to the application for a court order may be pre-date the involvement of the current social worker.

It is essential to read the whole file, not just transfer summaries. Previous files relating to the child or family should be retrieved and read.

Reading and note-taking are time-consuming and need to be scheduled into your personal timetable as described in chapter three.

## Make lists

You may wish to sketch out:

- a family tree or a genogram, including the wider family (the court is likely to find this useful)
- the family's history of involvement with social services (the reasons why this was initiated and by whom, frequency of interactions, services offered/provided, placements etc.)
- the family's involvement with other agencies, for example health, education, housing and child guidance
- the child's record on the child protection register
- the history of case conferences, planning meetings and decision-making
- steps taken to explore alternatives to court proceedings.

Summarise your own involvement with the child and family, including:

- the length of such involvement (and, if recent, the steps taken to familiarise yourself with the case)
- the number of contacts with individual members
- whether home visits were by appointment or unscheduled
- details of and reasons for appointments missed by family members or yourself.

Consider whether there are any documents on file which should be attached to your statement as an annex, for example:

- a contract or agreement with the family
- an assessment report
- a letter from the child or parent
- a letter from the social worker to the family explaining local authority concerns
- a letter to the child, if of sufficient age and understanding, explaining what is happening.

## Citing research

Citing research should be the exception rather than the rule. If you wish to refer to the theoretical basis for your opinion, identify the author of the cited research and the name of the publication in which it appeared. It is often preferable to refer to articles or books which provide an overview of findings on a particular subject, making you less susceptible to challenge on the basis that you singled out research which supports the local authority's position. Be aware of research which came to a different conclusion and draw it to the court's attention in your statement. You may be asked about such findings in cross-examination. If you are in any doubt about the advisability of research references, consult your legal adviser.

## Verify where possible

Are there any steps you should take to verify information for the court case? For example, where school absenteeism is an issue, have you asked the education welfare officer (also called education social workers) for a certification of attendance?

## Explain the reasons for the application

Where the local authority decides to make an application for a court order, you should:

- consult the parents, child and other relevant people
- explain why the local authority considers it necessary to make the application
- ensure that the parents understand the contents and purpose of the court documents if they have not yet instructed a solicitor
- provide those with parental responsibility with a list of solicitors on the Law Society Children Panel and a copy of any guidance your local authority may have which explains The Children Act and the courts.
- Give notice to those who are entitled to it, but without parental responsibility, and recommend that they seek legal advice .

The way in which this consultation process is carried out and the responses of the child, family and others to the local authority action should be described in the local authority's evidence. If you have decided not to consult a relevant person, for example because you believe it would place the child at greater risk to do so, then you should explain this in your statement.

## Be aware of special needs

Appropriate provision should be made for a child or parent with communications difficulties[1]. including language and literacy problems. Sensorily impaired children and adults may need information to be provided in a specific format. For the blind or visually impaired this could be braille, tape or large print. The deaf and hard of hearing have a range of communication needs depending on the type and age of onset of their hearing impairment.

When applying for an order, you should advise the court of the child or party's special needs in a supplement to the application. Your statement should describe the method(s) of communication employed and refer to any special steps or "special measures" the court should take to assist any party or witness with communication difficulties. This may include the use of an Intermediary at court to explain the questions to a witness and to help the witness convey the answer to the court.

---

1. *Department of Health (1991) The Children Act 1989 Guidance and Regulations Volume 3, Family Placements para. 2.71. HMSO.*

# Timetabling at court and within the local authority

The Children Act emphasises the need to avoid delay and requires the court to set a timetable that brings the case to a conclusion as quickly as possible in the best interests of the child. The timetable must allow for adequate preparation by participants but the scheduling of events should maintain a sense of urgency. The Protocol sets out best practice guidance for case management of public law Children Act cases.

This chapter:

- looks at the time limits set by the Protocol
- identifies ways in which social services can contribute to the court timetable
- suggests how you can manage and timetable the preparation of your written statement or report for court.

## Timetabling at court

**Delay is likely to be prejudicial**

> **SECTION 1(2)**
> **Delay in deciding any question about the child's upbringing is unlikely to prejudice the child's welfare.**

The Act recognises that, in general, the child's welfare is likely to suffer as a consequence of delay in proceedings. The court must set a timetable for any case involving children and issue directions to ensure the case is heard as quickly as possible (sections 11(1) and 32(1)). The Protocol specifies time limits for that timetable.

The overriding objective of the Protocol is to enable the court to deal with every care case

a) justly and expeditiously and with the minimum of delay

b) in ways which ensure , so far as is practicable, that

    (i) the parties are on an equal footing;

    (ii) the welfare of the children involved is safeguarded; and

    (iii) distress to all parties is minimised;

(c ) so far as is practicable, in ways which are proportionate

    (i) to the gravity and complexity of the issues; and

    (ii) to the nature and extent of the intervention proposed in the private and family life of the children and the adults involved.

The aims of the Protocol are to ensure:

- that care cases are dealt with in accordance with the overriding objective;

- that there are no unacceptable delays in the hearing and the determination of care cases; and

- that save in exceptional or unforeseen circumstances, every care case is finally determined within 40 weeks of the application being issued.

---

**The Protocol Route Map – The 6 Steps and their aims in italics**

**1. THE APPLICATION**                        **DAY 1 TO 3**

*To provide sufficient information about the Local Authority's case to enable:*
- *The parties and the court to identify the issues*
- *The court to make early welfare and case management decisions about the child*

**2. THE FIRST HEARING IN THE FAMILY**
**PROCEEDINGS COURT**              **ON OR BEFORE DAY 6**

*To decide what immediate steps are necessary to safeguard the welfare of the child by:*
- *Determining contested interim care order applications/with whom the child will live*
- *Identifying how to prevent delay*
- *Identifying the appropriate court*
- *Transferring to the appropriate court*

**3. ALLOCATION AND DIRECTIONS**      **BY DAY 11 in the Care**
                                                **Centre or BY DAY 15 in**
                                                **the High Court**

*To make provision for continuous and consistent judicial case management*

**4. CASE MANAGEMENT CONFERENCE ("CMC")**    **DAY 15 – DAY 60**

*To consider what case management directions are necessary*
- *To ensure that a fair hearing of the proceedings takes place*
- *To timetable the proceedings so that the Final Hearing is completed within or before the recommended hearing window*

**5. THE PRE HEARING REVIEW**                **BY WEEK 37**

*To identify and narrow the remaining issues between the parties and ensure that the Final Hearing is effective*

**6. THE FINAL HEARING**                        **BY WEEK 40**

*To determine the remaining issues between the parties*

The Protocol sets out 6 steps or stages in the case, also callled the "route map", for judges to follow when timetabling a case.

## 'Avoidable' delay

You should discuss with your legal adviser:

- the effect of delay on the child in question
- the availability of an expert witness on behalf of the local authority
- how the time limits set out in the 6 steps are going to be complied with.

Your statement should address the tension between the 'no delay' principle, the importance of assessing the child's needs, and how an assessment, if required, is likely to fit in with steps of the Protocol and the time limits set out in the Protocol.

## Provide time estimates

Before the first hearing (see below), it is your responsibility to provide your legal adviser with an estimate of the time required to file any additional written evidence such as the results of a social work assessment or an expert's report, and the final care plan . You should also indicate your availability for court hearings. Providing this information in advance will assist your legal adviser in contributing to the court timetable.

Your initial statement will be filed at the latest within 2 days of the application being issued at court. Normally, the court requires statements and reports to be filed in a logical sequence. This allows subsequent statements to comment on those which were filed earlier. In public law cases, the local authority files the first statement, though it may also file later evidence, the parents' statements usually follow the local authority's evidence and the report of the guardian (where one is appointed) is always the last scheduled submission. Court rules require that the report of the guardian is filed and served not less than fourteen days before the date fixed for the final hearing unless otherwise ordered[1].

## Notify legal adviser of potential delays

When a timetabled statement is filed late, time for response by other parties is reduced and it could result in a breach of the Protocol's overriding objective to ensure, so far as is practicable, that  the parties are on an equal footing and distress to all parties is minimised.  Filing evidence later than timetabled could put the other parties at a disadvantage, could lead to the final hearing being delayed and could be detrimental to the child/ren in the case.

You must comply with the court timetable to the best of your ability and submit your chronology and statement to the legal adviser in good time. It is the adviser's duty to ensure that documents are filed with the court and served on all parties. The court has powers to impose a wasted costs order as a penalty on the party responsible[2].

If there is a possibility that your chronology or statement will not be ready on time or you become aware that any other local authority evidence may be late (such as the report from an assessment), let your legal adviser know immediately. It is important that significant departures from the timetable be brought to the court's and the parties' attention as soon as is practicable. A further directions appointment may be needed.

## 'Purposeful' delay

In certain circumstances, the need to hold a final hearing as quickly as possible may be outweighed by other factors. Delay is 'purposeful' when specific activities are scheduled, with positive reasons for prolonging matters in the long-term interests of the child, for example a focused assessment, trial home stays or other reasonable attempt at rehabilitation.

When the court makes an interim care or interim supervision order it is possible for one of more parties to seek that the court makes a direction that the child be assessed (section 38 (6)). The House of Lords has said that:

"if the aims of the protocol are to be realised, it will always be necessary to think early and clearly about what assessments are indeed necessary to decide the case. In many cases, the local authority should be able to make its own core assessment and the child's guardian to make an independent assessment in the interests of the child. Further or other assessments should only be commissioned if they can bring something important to the case which neither the local authority nor the guardian is able to bring." [3]

If a particular assessment will extend the proceedings, the court will want to know the amount of time required and why this delay is in the child's best interests.

## The First Hearing in the Family Proceedings Court

All applications for care or supervision orders are commenced in the Family Proceedings Court (FPC). At the first hearing the court will decide what immediate steps are necessary such as:

- Whether it would be more appropriate for the case to be heard in a higher court
- Whether a contested interim care order hearing is required

Unless the case is transferred to a higher court or there is an urgent need for a contested interim care order hearing, the FPC will go on to address the case management checklist at the first hearing. The case management checklist is set out at Appendix A/3 of the Protocol (see Annex Two) and includes:

- Whether all the appropriate respondents have been identified and notified
- Whether any other person should be joined as a party
- Whether the grounds for making and ICO have been agreed
- What further documents need to be filed and when (including statements form the parties)
- The need, if any, for expert evidence and necessary directions such as permission for the expert to examine or interview the child for the purposes of reporting to court

- A date for the case management conference (CMC)
- A date for the pre hearing review (PHR)
- A date for the final hearing.

If the case is transferred to the County Court or to the High Court the judge in the higher court will follow the standard case management checklist at the directions hearing there.

The court controls the progress of the case by issuing directions and setting the timetable for filing evidence with the court. The court may make directions at the request of the parties or of its own motion.[4]

At each directions hearing the court will complete a 'Standard Directions Form' (Appendix A/1 of the Protocol, see Annex Two). Your legal adviser will be able to supply you with a copy after the hearing. Included in the form will be the name of the judge who will be responsible for the continuous case management of the case and the key dates such as the date of the case management conference, the pre hearing review, the date of the final hearing and the dates by which the parties must file their evidence.

## Timetabling within the local authority

### Personal plan for court work

The local authority witness should develop a personal timetable running alongside that of the court. This plan should include the scheduling of:

- dates on which your statements are due to be filed with the court (NB the filing date is not the same date for sending your statement to your legal adviser)
- time for reading files, preparation and writing the statement
- time for updating the chronology
- time for typing and review
- time for copying and distribution
- dates on which you are required to attend court
- consultations with the family
- consultation contributing to formulation of the care plan (or plans if there is more than one child in the proceedings)
- decision-making meetings (include booking the room and sending invitations)
- consultations and updating discussions with the guardian
- appointments with your legal adviser, including consultation prior to the final hearing.

## The manager's responsibilities

The local authority manager has a responsibility to:

- give priority to court work being undertaken by staff

- record the personal timetable of social worker witnesses on a unit-wide basis, so that the manager is aware of all team commitments to court work
- ensure that the witness has adequate time to prepare and write statements and update the chronology
- monitor compliance with the court timetable
- ensure that the care plan is based on a realistic allocation of resources
- review critically statements and reports.

1.  Rule 11(7), Family Proceedings Courts (Children Act 1989) Rules 1991; rule 4.11(7), Family Proceedings Rules 1991.

2.  In the matter of GS&H (Minors) (2000) 2 WLR 1007, (2000) 4 ALL ER 371.

3.  Baroness Hale of Richmond in Kent County Council v G and others [2005] UKHL 68.

4.  Rule 14(2), Family Proceedings Courts (Children Act 1989) Rules 1991; rule 4.14(2), Family Proceedings Rules 1991.

# The local authority legal adviser

Arrangements for the delivery of legal services vary among local authorities. Child protection work may be:

- handled 'in house' by a local authority lawyer
- assigned on an individual case basis to specialist solicitors in private practice
- contracted out by competitive tender.

Increasingly, lawyers (solicitors and barristers) handling this work have to account for their time in a way which has resource implications for the social services department. You should be aware of the arrangements for delivery of legal services in your area.

In individual cases, the legal adviser may brief a barrister from chambers to represent the local authority at court. Responsibility for day-to day management of the case remains with the legal adviser.

## Source of independent legal advice

The local authority legal adviser works closely with social services and other agencies involved in child protection. The adviser acts on the instructions of the social services department and should always be consulted before proceedings are begun. There may well be a "gatekeeper" in the local authority who determines if and when the legal advisers should be consulted. The legal advisers may require formal written instructions when they are consulted.

## Legal adviser's duties

The legal adviser's primary duties are to the court and the interests of the child. The adviser's client is the local authority but the day-to-day working relationship is with the Director of Social Services, acting through local managers and social workers.

Certain common principles apply, irrespective of local provisions for legal services. It is the responsibility of the legal adviser to:

- maintain the integrity of the local authority before the court
- examine the local authority's case at an early stage
- attend case conferences and formal planning meetings whenever possible
- ensure that all relevant information is before the court and the other parties
- ensure that the statement accurately represents the witness's evidence and that the witness understands what is written in the statement and signs the statement
- meet strict timetable requirements.

The local authority should be an equal participant in informed discussions about the court timetable. In order for the local authority's requirements fully to be taken into consideration by the court adequate information must be presented to the court. The local authority legal adviser should:

- Complete the Protocol's Case Management Questionnaire where required to do so by the court in advance of a Case Management Conference hearing

- help the court fix hearings when witnesses are available by supplying the court with a completed witness non-availability form as found in the Protocol

- consult with those involved to provide time estimates for the submission of statements, expert reports, the updated chronology and the care plan/s

- consult with the other parties about the timetable well in advance of a directions hearing

- develop a draft timetable for consideration by the court.

In exceptional circumstances, the legal adviser's duties to the court and the interests of the child transcend those of social services and the client authority. For example, any instructions from social services that documentation or information relevant to the case should not be disclosed is likely to be challenged by the legal adviser.

## Resolving disputes

In the unlikely event of a dispute arising between the social services department and the legal adviser concerning disclosure or the management of the case, the issue should be addressed at a senior level in both organisations.

## Document bundles

Court guidelines have been issued[1] regarding legal representatives' preparation of document bundles for hearings. Social workers should be aware of the legal adviser's responsibilities with respect to indexing, pagination etc. and the time requirements for bundle preparation.

**Figure 2: Court structure for proceedings under the Children Act 1989**

**HOUSE OF LORDS**
- **Appeals from Court of Appeal**

**COURT OF APPEAL**
- **Appeals from High Court and county court**

**HIGH COURT (Family Division)**
- **Public and private law cases involving complex points or issues of law**
- **Private law applications made by children**

- Appeals from the family proceedings court
- Inherent jurisdiction

## COUNTY COURT

**Care Centre**

*Circuit Judge/District Judge of the Principal Registry in London*

- Transferred public law cases
- Applications when there are pending proceedings, or to vary, extend or discharge existing orders of the court
- Private law cases

*District Judge*

- Directions in public and private law cases
- Transfer applications refused by family proceedings court referred for reconsideration
- Powers to make certain preliminary or limited and agreed orders in public and private law cases

**Family Hearing Centre**

*Circuit Judge*

- Private law cases

*District Judge*

- Directions in private law cases
- Powers to make preliminary and agreed orders in private law cases

## FAMILY PROCEEDINGS COURT

- Most public law cases are commenced here
- Private law cases may be commenced here

*Reproduced with kind permission from Pizzey S. and Davis J. (1995) A Guide for Guardians ad Litem in Public Law Proceedings under the Children Act 1989. Department of Health. HMSO.*

---

1   Practice Direction (Family Proceedings: Court Bundles) [2000] 1 FCR 521, [2000] 1 FLR 536 issued on
    10th March 2000 by Dame Elizabeth Butler-Sloss the then President of the Family Division.

# Working with experts and other key participants

This chapter describes the responsibilities of the local authority:

- **to provide information to assist the court when an assessment or expert examination is under consideration**
- **to liaise with other participants in the court process, namely:**

  **the guardian and the interpreter (if required)**

# Referral for assessment or expert examination

## The expert's duty

The Protocol makes it very clear that an expert in family proceedings has an overriding duty to the court that takes precedence over any obligation to the person from whom he has received instructions or by whom he is paid.

## Is an expert necessary?

It is essential that the parties and the court are clear about the purpose of an assessment, how it will serve the best interests of the child and in what way it will add to already available evidence. Is the assessment necessary to resolve issues about the threshold conditions or the care plan? What aspects of these require an expert opinion? Lack of confidence in social work evidence can lead to the commissioning of expert reports which confirm the authority's earlier submissions. This can contribute to delays in reaching final hearings.

## Pre-hearing enquiries

Once the application has been made, the child cannot be medically or psychiatrically examined or otherwise assessed for the purpose of preparing expert evidence for use in the proceedings without leave of the court[1]. If the child is of sufficient understanding, he or she is entitled to refuse such an examination.

Where the local authority wishes to refer the child, family or both for assessment, before this matter is raised at court hearing the local authority should enquire about the availability of those who might carry out the assessment. Consultations should also be held with the other parties, particularly the guardian who advises the court on this issue. The court's permission is required to instruct the expert and to send court papers to the expert.

The local authority should tell the court:

- the name, discipline, qualification and expertise of the expert (by way of CV where possible)
- the expert's availability to undertake the work
- the relevance of the expert evidence sought to be adduced to the issues in the proceedings and the specific questions upon which it is proposed the expert should give an opinion (including the relevance of any diverse cultural or religious contexts)
- the timetable for the report
- the responsibility for instructing the expert
- whether or not the expert evidence can properly be obtained by the joint instruction of the expert by two or more parties
- whether the expert evidence can properly be obtained by only one party (eg on behalf of the child)
- whether it is necessary for more than one expert in the same discipline to be instructed by more than party
- why the expert evidence proposed cannot be given by social services undertaking a core assessment or by the guardian in accordance with their different statutory duties
- the likely cost of the report on both an hourly and global(overall) basis
- the proposed apportionment of costs of jointly instructed experts as between the local authority and the publicly funded parties (ie the guardian and the parents who are usually legally aided)

All of this information must be set out in the Case Management Questionnaire and filed with the court at least 2 days before any application is to be made[2].

The Children Act Advisory Committee recommended the use of a core curriculum vitae for an expert witness[3].

## The letter of instruction

Guidance on what the letter of instruction should contain is set out in the Protocol Appendix C: Code of Guidance for Expert Witnesses in Family Proceedings, paragraph 3 Letter of Instruction (see Annex Two).

The Protocol, Appendix C, paragraph 4, sets out guidance on the content and form of the expert's report. The expert's report should be addressed to the court.

If there are supplementary questions about the report that seek to clarify matters in the report, they should be put in writing to the parties no later than 5 days after receipt of the report. The Protocol, Appendix C, paragraph 5, gives guidance on experts discussions/meetings and arranging for the expert to attend court. Making the arrangements is the responsibility of the party instructing the expert.

Once the hearing is concluded it is the responsibility of the solicitor instructing the expert to provide feedback to the expert by way of a letter telling them of the outcome of the case, and the use made by the Court of the expert's opinion. (The Protocol, Appendix C, paragraph 7).

## Joint referral preferable

It is preferable to have one expert jointly instructed and it would be unrealistic and unnecessary for the courts to permit the other parties to obtain 'mirror' reports in every discipline. The court will expect parties to try to agree a single programme of joint assessment. However when the issue that the expert has to address is of central importance to the judge's finding, for example where it concerns pivotal medical evidence which by its nature is not easily challengeable in the absence of other expert evidence, the court should be slow to decline an application for a second expert.[4]

When parties consent to a joint referral, the letter of instruction should be circulated for agreement and the statements and other documents to be disclosed to the expert should be listed in the letter of referral. The expert should set out in the report the substance of all material instructions (verbal or in writing). Consent to a joint referral does not invariably involve sharing the cost of the assessment, which should be addressed separately by the parties' representatives. Guidelines have been set down by the court with regard to how the costs of the joint instruction should be apportioned.[5]

## The timetable

When considering the instruction of an expert the court will make directions regarding:

- the matters to be addressed in the expert's report
- authority to disclose relevant papers to the expert
- the date when the report of the assessment is to be filed with the court
- a directions appointment after the completion of the assessment to reassess the case timetable, decide what further evidence is required (expert and otherwise) and obtain further directions for a speedy hearing
- a date for the final hearing, if this has not been fixed already
- whether or not the expert has permission to see the child.

## Timeliness of expert reports

Late filing of expert reports and assessment is a significant cause of delay, often requiring final hearings to be rescheduled.

The referral letter should emphasise the importance of filing the report in accordance with the timetable set by the court and the need to comply with the Protocol. The letter should be accompanied by an indexed, paginated bundle including:

- A copy of the order (or those parts of the order) which gives permission for the instruction of expert immediately the order becomes available
- An agreed list of essential reading
- All new documentation when it is filed and regular updates to the list of documents provided or to the index to the paginated bundle
- A copy of the Protocol drawing particular attention to the Code of Guidance for Expert Witnesses in Family Proceedings (Appendix C of the Protocol).

The expert should be requested to notify the appropriate legal adviser at the earliest opportunity if the report is likely to be late. It is not acceptable for the expert to give such notice on or just before the due date.

The court has the power to impose a wasted costs order if late reports cause adjournment[6].

## Informing the child and family of the outcome

The conclusions of the expert report or assessment may be deeply distressing to the child and family. The letter of instruction should clarify who has responsibility for informing the child and family of the outcome of the assessment.

Example of an excerpt from a commissioning letter to a psychologist:

'Towards the close of your psychological assessment, it would be most helpful if you would allow time to discuss your conclusion and recommendations with Mr and Mrs Taylor and, if appropriate, with Simone (aged 9) and to incorporate their responses into your report. If they have not been informed of your conclusion and recommendations, please make this clear in your report to the court.'

## Keeping the expert up-to-date

It should be established among the parties who has responsibility to supply all statements filed with the court (including the care plan) to the expert who may be asked to comment on them while giving evidence. It will usually be the responsibility of the solicitor who sent the original letter of instruction to ensure that the expert receives copies of all further documents filed if they are relevant to the expert's work. A lot of time can be wasted if it is discovered later, at a hearing or at the experts' meeting for example, that the expert does not have the up-to-date papers.

## Liaison with other participants

The social worker may have contact with other key individuals involved in the court process:

- the guardian
- the interpreter.

You should be aware of their duties and any responsibilities you have in assisting them to carry out their role.

# The guardian

In public law cases, the child's interests are usually represented by the children's guardian who is employed by CAFCASS (Children and Family Court Advisory and Support Service). This is a public body independent of the local authority. The guardian should be appointed by the court at an early stage in line with the timescale set out in Step 1 of the Protocol.

### The guardian's duties

It is the guardian's responsibility[7] to:

- safeguard the interests of the child
- carry out an investigation and advise the court of the result including making the child's views known to the court.

To fulfil this role, the guardian:

- appoints a solicitor to act for the child (unless one is already appointed by the court)
- gives advice to the child in a way the child can understand
- discusses the issues with all the parties before the case is heard
- gathers evidence
- attends all hearings unless excused
- provides the court with an impartial written report recommending what is best for the child.

The guardian advises the court about:

- the timetable
- the appointment of an expert
- whether anyone else who would be likely to safeguard the interests of the child should be involved in the proceedings
- whether the child is of sufficient understanding to refuse medical or psychiatric examination or other assessment
- the wishes of the child
- the appropriate forum for the proceedings
- any other relevant matter.

# Attendance at meetings

Local authorities usually have a local policy on the invitation of guardians to planning meetings and case conferences. Where family members are present, in order to maintain independence, the guardian usually attends only as an observer and may withdraw during decision-making and when legal advice is given. You should keep the guardian informed of any developments, particularly those that affect the child's placement or contact.

### Full access to case records

Section 42 authorises the guardian to examine and take copies of local authority records concerning the child who is the subject of the application. This includes minutes of case conferences, planning meetings and documents relating to any potential adoption or adopters. Social workers and guardians should be aware that if a guardian takes a copy of a record and refers to it in the report, the record can become evidence and copies may need to be provided to other parties. The guardian's right of access does not however extend to legal advice given to the social worker by the local authority legal advisers. Records of legal advice are 'privileged' and it is good practice to keep such correspondence separate from the case records to avoid confusion.

The guardian's report is submitted to the court in accordance with directions but usually at least fourteen days before the final hearing. The guardian has a responsibility to comment on the local authority care plan and this should be provided to the guardian as soon as it is available.

### Avoiding duplication of appointments

Pending court proceedings create a lot of extra pressure for children, families and foster carers. Many additional activities may be involved such as assessment appointments and supervised contact sessions. Social workers and guardians should notify each other of their appointments with children and families so that scheduling conflicts can be avoided. Note also that the solicitor appointed for an older child is likely to make visits to see the child independently of the guardian.

# The interpreter

### Interpreter must be impartial

When you do not speak the language of the child or of any party or they are hearing impaired and their full participation would not otherwise be possible, an interpreter must be used in interviews. It is essential that an interpreter remains impartial and professional and has an understanding of welfare or legal work. The use of family members, particularly children, is inappropriate. Find an interpreter who speaks the family's mother tongue rather than a language or dialect in which they can 'get by' or arrange a signer through the Institute for the Deaf. .

Give the interpreter sufficient information about the assignment, including the terminology, concepts and procedures involved, to allow for preparation. Make sure that the interpreter understands that they have a duty to keep all matters discussed confidential.

Allow enough time. During an interpreted interview, everything has to be said twice. Ask the interpreter to speak in the first person when translating. Give full, clear explanations of concepts and procedures. A non-specialist interpreter may not know the precise meaning of some terms and indeed, they may not exist in the same form in the other language. Signing for the deaf is very tiring and reasonable breaks should be allowed for.

## Interpreters at court

Make sure that the interpreter has sufficient information about the court hearing (where to meet and at what time, etc) and clarify with the parties whose responsibility it is to pay for the interpreter[8].

Additional time must be allowed for court hearings when interpretation is necessary.

## CAFCASS Legal and the Official Solicitor

A small proportion of cases are referred to CAFCASS Legal if an exceptionally complex or controversial issue arises. Sometimes it will be appropriate for the Attorney General or the Official Solicitor to be involved. In such case the local authority legal advisor will liase with their offices in the first instance. If one of the parents appears to lack mental capacity you should inform your legal adviser as soon as possible. If the parent does lack mental capacity, the Official Solicitor must be appointed to represent him/her and the proceedings will have to be transferred up to the County Court for this to be done.

---

1    Rule 18(1), Family Proceedings Courts (Children Act 1989) Rules 1991; rule 4.18(1), Family Proceedings Rules 1991.

2    the Protocol .

3    Annual Report 1993/94, pp. 24-25.

4    GW and PW v Oldham Metropolitan Borough Council [2005] EWCA Civ 1247.

5    Calderdale Metropolitan Borough v S (2005) FLR 751.

6    R v Nottingham County Council [1993] 1 FCR 576 .

7    Rule 11(4), Family Proceedings Courts (Children Act 1989) Rules 1991; rule 4.11(4), Family Proceedings Rules 1991 and s 41 (2) (b) The Children Act 1989.

8    For information about the National Register of Public Service Interpreters, go to www.nrpsi.co.uk or call 020 7940 3166.

# Public law applications

This chapter deals with applications for:

- emergency protection orders (section 44)
- child assessment orders (section 43)
- care or supervision orders (section 31)
- discharge and variation of care and supervision orders (section 39)
- secure accommodation orders (section 25)

The power of the court to order an investigation is dealt with in chapter seven.
Contact and related issues are covered in chapter thirteen.

## Emergency protection orders

> **Section 44**
>
> (1) Where any person applies for an emergency protection order, the court may make an order if it is satisfied
>
>    (a) there is reasonable cause to believe that the child is likely to suffer significant harm if
>
>       (i) he is not removed or
>
>       (ii) he does not remain in the place in which he is then being accommodated; or
>
>    (b) in the case of an application made by a local authority
>
>       (i) enquiries about the child are being made under section 47(1)(b); and
>
>       (ii) those enquiries are being frustrated by access to the child being unreasonably refused and that the applicant has reasonable cause to believe that access to the child is required as a matter of urgency.

## Purpose

An emergency protection order gives the applicant parental responsibility for the duration of the order (section 44 (4) ( c)). The applicant must exercise that parental responsibility:

- to safeguard and promote the welfare of the child
- where necessary, by removing the child to accommodation provided, or
- by preventing the child's removal from his or her present accommodation.

The court may make directions for contact with the child and medical or psychiatric examination or assessment.

## Why is an emergency order necessary?

Wherever possible, legal advice should be obtained before seeking an emergency protection order. Explain to the court why the child's safety is immediately threatened and why the child is at risk of harm if not removed from where the child is now or not kept where the child is now. The court will only make an emergency protection order in extremely urgent cases where there is a genuine need for emergency legal intervention.

## Specify significant harm

Describe the significant harm suffered or why it is reasonable to believe that the child is likely to suffer significant harm. If there is a suspected non-accidental injury, a medical report should be obtained. (For further discussion of 'significant harm', see section 31 applications below.)

You will probably not be able to address all relevant issues in writing. You should be prepared to provide oral evidence to the court.

## Describe any consultation

Although the circumstances are likely to require urgent attention, consultation with other professionals who are closely involved will assist in a measured approach. If consultation has taken place, this should be reflected.

## Proposed contact to be reasonable

If an emergency protection order is made, the local authority must allow parents reasonable contact with their child through visits and phone calls unless this puts the child's welfare at risk. The local authority may only refuse contact if it is satisfied that the need is urgent and it is necessary to do so in order to safeguard or promote the child's welfare. The court may give directions in respect of contact which is, or is not, to be allowed between the child and any named person (section 44(6)(a)). These directions may impose conditions (section 44(8)). Subject to any such directions, the authority must allow reasonable contact with persons specified in section 44(13).

## Action following the order

Be prepared to tell the court what steps the local authority intends to take following the making of the order regarding placement, treatment or other aspect of the care plan.

An application for an emergency protection order can either be made with or without advance notice. Without notice applications should be made only in the most compelling circumstances and if the situation is considered to require immediate action and there is good reason for not giving notice such as the likelihood of danger to the child. There is a difference between the need for immediate action and the need to proceed without notice. The court may insist that you give notice by telephone to enable the parent or solicitor to be heard. In the Family Proceedings Court permission of the Court Clerk is required for an application without notice to be heard and permission is not lightly given. If the hearing proceeds ex parte (ie. with only the local authority present), it is doubly important that the local authority makes every effort to verify information relied upon in the application and identifies any information not so verified. The local authority must provide full and frank information to assist the court's decision making.

## Child assessment orders

> **Section 43**
>
> (1) **On the application of a local authority or authorised person for a child assessment order, the court may make the order if it is satisfied.**
>
> (a) **that the applicant has reasonable cause to suspect that the child is suffering, or is likely to suffer significant harm**
>
> (b) **an assessment of the state of the child's health or development, or of the way in which he has been treated, is required to enable the applicant to determine whether or not the child is suffering, or is likely to suffer, significant harm; and**
>
> (c) **it is unlikely that such an assessment will be made, or be satisfactory, in the absence of an order under this section.**

The child assessment order enables a medical, psychiatric or social work assessment of the child to be made where significant harm is suspected and the parents have refused to cooperate. The assessment may last up to a maximum of 7 days from the date specified in the order. It is likely that any application will have been preceded by a section 47 investigation.

The application should be made with advance notice to those with Parental Responsibility (section 42 (11)).

Tell the court:

- about the local authority's investigation into the welfare of the child

- what steps were taken to persuade the parents to cooperate with the investigation

- what kind of assessment is sought (it may be of a medical or psychiatric nature) and the questions to be addressed

- the person or institution that will carry out the assessment

- when the assessment will start, how long it will last and whether the child needs to stay away from home overnight (the court will order this only if absolutely necessary)

- the length of the order sought (the maximum is seven days)

- the child's view (the order does not take away the child's own right to refuse medical examination, so long as he or she is sufficiently able to understand the situation).

Example of excerpt from an application for a child assessment order:

'Doctor G. Crawford, consultant community physician, will conduct an immediate physical examination of the children at their home if we can see them today. She has suggested that in light of the family history, the court grants permission for a full skeletal survey. If the children appear fit and well we do not propose to carry this out today. However, if there is superficial evidence of injuries, Dr Crawford may feel it is necessary for the children to be examined further at hospital. We therefore request a child assessment order for 36 hours, starting today.'

## Are there grounds for an EPO?

The court will not make a child assessment order if it is satisfied that there are grounds for making an emergency protection order and that it ought to make an emergency protection order (section 43 (4) (a) and section 42 (4) (b)). Consequently child assessment orders are rare.

**Figure 3: Children Act orders giving authority for temporary removal of a child**

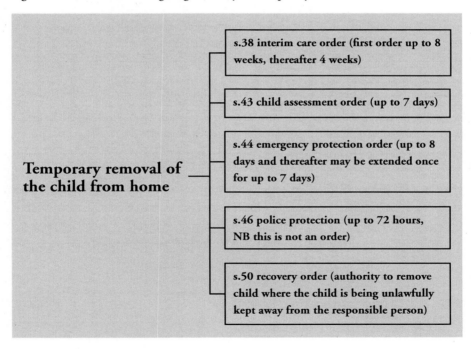

## Care or supervision orders

> **Section 31(2)**
>
> **A court may only make a care or supervision order if it is satisfied:**
>
> (a) **that the child concerned is suffering, or is likely to suffer significant harm; and**
>
> (b) **that the harm, or likelihood of harm, is attributable to**
>
> > (i) **the care given to the child, or likely to be given to him if the order were not made, not being what it would be reasonable to expect a parent to give him; or**
> >
> > (ii) **the child's being beyond parental control.**

## The threshold criteria

See the 'Significant Harm Criteria' flow-chart at the end of the discussion of section 31(2). It is important to seek legal advice as to whether the threshold criteria are satisfied.

The court should be informed about:

- the harm suffered or the reasons for the likelihood of harm, and whether this is attributable to:

  ill-treatment, which may include sexual, physical or emotional abuse or

  the impairment of physical or mental health or

  the impairment of physical, intellectual, emotional, social or behavioural development.

- Significant harm may also occur where a child sees or hears ill-treatment of another for example witnessing domestic violence. The court should be informed if this is the case.

## Identify those responsible for causing harm

- the identity of those responsible for causing harm to the child, if known and how it is known. Where ill-treatment is alleged, this must be proved on the balance of probabilities in other words the court must be satisfied that it is more likely than not that the ill-treatment occurred as alleged. The party (usually the local authority) seeking to show that the harm occurred must prove it occurred; it is not for the parents to prove that it did not occur. The more serious the allegation the stronger the evidence must be to prove it.[1]

## Children with special needs may require a higher standard of parenting care

- the parenting needs of the child in question rather than an average child (a subjective test). If the child has particular difficulties this could require a higher standard of care than for the average child[2].

# Compare the child's health or development with that of a 'similar' child

- where facts relate to health or development, what could reasonably be expected of a similar child. The standard should only be that which it is reasonable to expect for the child in question, rather than the best that could possibly be achieved (an objective test). The court may take account of environmental, social and cultural characteristics[3].

# Is the harm 'significant'?

- whether the harm is serious (such as a skull fracture) or is significant because of its implications (for example, a cigarette burn). 'Minor shortcomings in health care or minor deficits in physical, psychological or social development' should not require compulsory intervention unless cumulatively they are having, or are likely to have, serious and lasting effects upon the child[4].

# Is the harm attributable to 'care given' or 'likely to be given'?

- how the parent has exercised parental responsibility in the past, and any plans for future care of the child[5]
- the relevant date for the court to determine whether the threshold criteria were satisfied[6].

**Example illustrating the issue of relevant dates:**

Consider the case of a child who was the subject of an EPO two years ago. On that occasion, the local authority after investigation decided to take no further action. Three months ago, another EPO was obtained by the local authority based on concerns of ill-treatment. Care proceedings were immediately instituted and a number of interim care orders were made. The final hearing is today. The Court will look at whether the threshold criteria were satisfied on the date when the more recent EPO was obtained. The court cannot look at the circumstances relating to the EPO two years ago because of the break in child protection procedures. However, if the court decides that the criteria have been satisfied then in deciding what order to make, if any, it will look at the whole history of the case including the EPO incident two years ago.

# Distinguish care and supervision orders

The threshold criteria for the making of a care order are the same as those for a supervision order. However, the content of the two orders are completely different and the appropriate choice of order requires an evaluation of future risk. If a supervision order is made, the role of the local authority is limited as parental responsibility is exercised solely by the parent/s. The local authority should describe the details of parental supervision and cooperation on which it relies to safeguard and protect the child and should set out what conditions, if any, it wishes to attach to the order. Conditions may apply to the child or to the responsible person. Conditions imposed should be set out in the order[7].

On an application for a care order the court may make a supervision order and vice versa (section 31 (5)).

**Figure 4: Significant harm criteria**

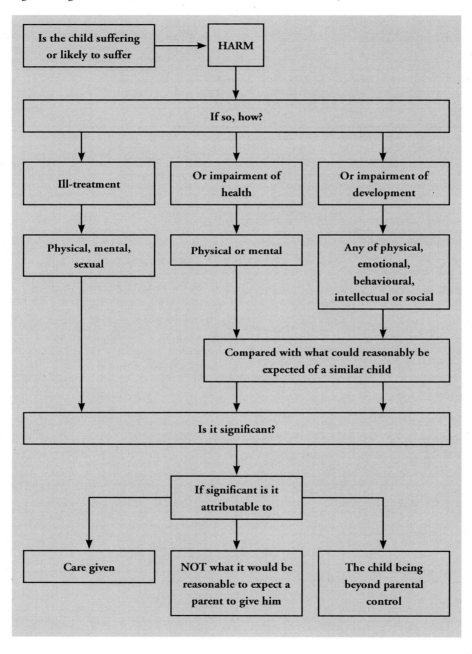

*Reproduced with kind permission from Adcock M., White R. and Hollows A. (1991) Significant Harm: its management and outcome. Significant Publications.*

# Why an order is necessary

You will also need to explain to the court why an order is necessary rather than simply providing support services under the local authority's duties towards children in need.

# Discharge and variation of care or supervision orders

*SECTION 39*

(1) **A care order may be discharged by the court on the application of any person who has parental responsibility for the child, the child himself or the local authority designated by the care order.**

(2) **A supervision order may be discharged by the court on the application of any person who has parental responsibility for the child, the child himself, or the supervisor.**

(4) **Where a care order is in force, the court may, on application of any person entitled to apply for the order to be discharged, substitute a supervision order for the care order.**

When the application is to discharge an order, the risk to be considered is that at the date of the discharge hearing. The court will be concerned with evidence of recent harm and assessment of current risk. The welfare of the child is paramount and the court will have regard to the welfare checklist.

When the application is to replace a supervision order with a care order, the court has to make a fresh finding on the facts. The court will conduct a full hearing, re-examining the evidence against the criteria in section 31.

# Secure accommodation

**(NB: This Section of the Handbook does not apply to applications in the Youth Court during criminal proceedings).**

*SECTION 25*

(1) **A child being looked after by the local authority may not be placed or kept in secure accommodation unless it appears:**

(a) **that**

(i) **he has a history of absconding and is likely to abscond from any other description of accommodation and**

(ii) **if he absconds, he is likely to suffer significant harm; or**

(b) **that if he is kept in any other description of accommodation he is likely to injure himself or other persons.**

## Statutory criteria

A child need not be the subject of a care order before being placed in secure accommodation, but if anyone with parental responsibility objects and there is no care order, the child must not be so placed. The maximum length of time during which a child can be kept in secure accommodation before the case must be taken to court is 72 hours in total, whether or not consecutive, in a period of 28 consecutive days. A statement must be produced before the first hearing (a chronology is likely to be particularly useful).

The court must be informed of:

- the child's history of absconding
- the likelihood of absconding from any other type of accommodation
- the likelihood of significant harm to the child if absconding occurs, or
- the ground for believing that the child is likely to injure himself or other persons if kept in any other type of accommodation.

## History of Absconding

When considering a child's history of absconding, factors to be considered include:

- whether the child injured himself or others
- any harm that the child suffered while absconding
- the reason for running away
- the child's associates
- over what period the absconding has taken place and with what frequency
- did the child commit any offences
- where the child ran to (did the child remain nearby)
- did the child return voluntarily
- whether the child's behaviour is a reflection of the pattern of the institution (including the frequency and reasons for the absconding of other residents).

## Order mandatory if statutory criteria satisfied

If the statutory criteria are satisfied, then it is mandatory for the court to make the order. If the criteria are not satisfied, no order can be made however much the child's welfare may seem to require it.

## Views of child and family

Before making a decision in relation to any child being looked after, the local authority has a general duty to ascertain the child's wishes and feelings and those of the parent, other persons with parental responsibility and any other relevant person (section 22).

The local authority must ensure that the child:

- understands the nature of the application and the purpose of the hearing
- has time to prepare their defence to the application
- has access to free legal advice if required[8]
- has the opportunity to question witnesses
- has an interpreter if necessary

The child who is the subject of the application is usually brought to court for the hearing.

A child who is the subject of a care order should be helped by the local authority to contact a solicitor who can represent the child in these proceedings. Otherwise a list of Law Society Children's Panel solicitors should be given to the child. When an application for a secure accommodation is made the court will appoint a guardian for the child – usually the same one as in the care proceedings.

## Physical and mental health

The local authority should provide information about:

- the child's physical and mental health (section 25(1)(b))
- whether the child's capabilities or understanding are permanently or temporarily impaired by medication, learning difficulty or psychiatric illness
- the ability of local child and adolescent services to assist the child.

## Length of order considered separately

The court must consider the length of the order as a separate issue. The local authority should state how long it considers the order should last and may refer to the welfare checklist in this context. Upon a first application, a secure accommodation order can be made for a maximum of three months. On a second application, the maximum duration is six months. Instead of making a full order at the first hearing, the court may make a 28 day interim secure order which counts towards the length of the final order. The child's interests are best served if interim and final orders are kept as short as possible.

## Describe clearly the objectives of secure accommodation

The court should be informed about:

- the details of the care plan
- the aims to be served by secure accommodation and to what extent restriction of liberty is consistent with the care plan
- how those providing the secure accommodation meet these aims
- to what extent these aims can be achieved within the maximum initial period of the order.

## The choice of secure unit

With the needs of the child in mind and in the context of the care plan, the characteristics of the proposed placement should be described. Factors may include:

- the age, gender and race of other residents
- the number being detained for certain grave crimes under section 53 Children and Young Persons Act 1933
- the number of children on remand
- the number of Police and Criminal Evidence Act 1984 detainees
- whether, in the case of placement in a psychiatric hospital, there is sufficient evidence that the child suffers from a psychiatric illness.

## Secure accommodation is a last resort

Secure accommodation is not a form of punishment and must not be used as a 'breathing space', because no other placement is available or because the child is being a nuisance. The local authority must:

- demonstrate that all alternatives have been comprehensively considered or pursued and rejected, including a thorough review of local facilities[9]
- describe what other forms of accommodation have been tried
- describe whether alternative forms of accommodation exist.

Children usually become the subject of secure accommodation applications after intervention by various agencies. Describe any process of consultation with others and the multi-agency approach.

---

1   *Re H and Others (Minors) (Sexual Abuse: Standard of Proof) [1996] 1 All ER 1, Re H and R (child Sexual Abuse: Standard of Care) [1996] 1 FLR 80.*

2   *Adcock M., White R. and Hollows A. (1991) Significant Harm : its management and outcome. Significant Publications p. 9.*

3   *Department of Health (1991) The Children Act 1989 Guidance and Regulations Volume 1, Court Orders para. 3.20. HMSO.*

4   *Department of Health (1991) The Children Act 1989 Guidance and Regulations Volume 1, Court Orders para. 3.21. HMSO.*

5   *Department of Health (1991) The Children Act 1989 Guidance and Regulations Volume 1, Court Orders para. 3.23. HMSO.*

6   *Re M (a Minor) (Care Order: Threshold Conditions) [1994] 2 AC 424, [1994] 3 WLR 558, [1994] 3 All ER 298, [1994] FLR 577 (HL)*

7   *Re T (A Minor) (Care Order: Conditions) [1994] 2 FLR 423 (CA).*

8   *Re C (Secure Accommodation Order, Representation) [2001] EWCA Civ 458].*

9   *The local authority is under a specific duty to avoid the need for children in their area to be placed in secure accommodation (Schedule 2, para. 7(c)).*

# Private law: court-ordered enquiries

**7**

This chapter describes the preparation of reports in response to court-ordered investigations under sections 7 and 37. Although section 37 enquiries can be ordered by the court in public law cases, most originate in private law proceedings.

In private law matters, the court may direct Social Services to provide information concerning the child's welfare, for example where there is a dispute between the parties about the residence of the child, contact or parental responsibility.

When you prepare a report in a private law matter at the request of the court, the same standards should be applied to the contents as those you apply when you write witness statements. Treat it seriously, do not treat it as an invitation, it is a court order.

Local authority legal advisers are not always notified automatically of requests for reports from the court but you should still consult the adviser if you have any questions.

## Welfare reports

> *SECTION 7*
>
> (1) **A court considering any question with respect to a child under the Children Act may ask a probation officer, local authority or other appropriate person such as the NSPCC, to report to the court on such matters relating to the welfare of that child as are required to be dealt with in the report**
>
> (3) **The report may be made orally or in writing as the court requires.**

## Purpose of s. 7 enquiry

Section 7 reports may be prepared by CAFCASS officers, social workers or the NSPCC. In most cases, the report is prepared by a social worker only where there is current or recent involvement with the family. The general principles of the Children Act apply.

The purpose of a section 7 enquiry is to provide the court with information and advice as to what (if any) orders should be made to promote the child's welfare. This does not mean that you must conduct a full 'core assessment'. Appendix F of the Protocol (see Annex Two) provides an "Aide memoire" that sets out the stages for assessments. It is not your role to resolve disputes when preparing a welfare report, though you may identify opportunities for helping the parties to reach agreement.

## Scope

A Practice Direction[1] advises courts to specify the nature of the enquiries which they wish the court welfare officer to undertake. Nevertheless, section 7 reports are often ordered without clear reasons being given by the court. Even if the court has identified specific areas of concern, you are not prevented from bringing other relevant matters to its attention. Early consideration should be given to the need for expert evidence in such a case.

If you have any question about the scope or nature of the enquiry, you can request further directions from the court. This may not require a hearing as some requests for directions can be dealt with by letter (seek the advice of the local authority legal advisor).

As in other enquiries concerning the best interests of the child, you should advise the parties that your discussions with them are not confidential and may be disclosed in your report. Section 7(4) provides that any matter referred to in the report, whether hearsay or opinion, is admissible so long as it is relevant. Nevertheless, where hearsay evidence is relied upon, this should be made explicit in the report as should the source of the information. The court needs information and advice to make judgements as to the weight to be given to hearsay evidence.

## Relevant sources

Information may already be held about the child, parties or prospective members of the household in:

- the local authority child protection register
- medical records
- school/education records
- social work records
- probation records
- police records.

Adult subjects should always be informed if a check is being made and be given an opportunity to comment on the accuracy of any factual information revealed about them. The report should confirm whether this has occurred.

## Planning your enquiry

Consider whether it is appropriate to:

- see the parties separately and/or together
- visit each party at home
- contact other relevant agencies such as the school, doctor and health visitor
- see each child alone and with siblings
- see each child with both parents

- see each child with each parent
- see any other significant carers
- see the new partners of a parent.

Where difficulties occur, discuss them with the court and, if necessary, ask for further directions.

## The child's wishes and feelings

> When conducting a section 7 enquiry, there is a strong presumption that you should see the child. If you do not do so, give your reasons in the report.

During meetings with the child:

- give the child the opportunity to express wishes and feelings
- do not allow a child to be forced to express a view or to take responsibility for decisions which properly belong to adults.

## Parties have a choice

Joint meetings should be encouraged but cannot be compelled. Inform the parties in writing that:

- they are free to choose whether to attend a joint meeting or to be seen separately
- whatever choice they make will not be to the detriment of their case
- they should take legal advice if unsure of their position.

In cases in which violence between the parties has been alleged, a joint interview must not be convened if it can reasonably be foreseen that the safety or well-being of a child or either party might be jeopardised.

## Children at risk

> During the course of your enquiries, if it becomes apparent that a child may be at risk of significant harm, the concern must be followed up and reported immediately in accordance with local child protection procedures. The court must be advised of the situation and you should suspend the enquiry pending further directions from the court.
>
> Practice Direction 24 February 1984 [1984] FLR 356 states that welfare reports must be endorsed with the words:
>
> This report has been prepared for the court and should be treated as confidential. It must not be shown nor its contents revealed to any person other than a party or a legal adviser to such a party. Such legal adviser may make use of the report in connection with an application for legal aid.

On completion of the report, you should send it to your legal advisers only who will file it with the court. It is a matter for the court to decide to whom the section 7 report will be disclosed.

All legal advisers who supply copies of section 7 reports to parties should make it absolutely clear that the report is confidential and to show it to anyone else is contempt unless the court gives permission.[2]

In the absence of a direction, your report should be submitted to the court 14 days before the hearing. You need not attend the hearing unless required to do so by the court.

## Contents of the s.7 report

Points to be addressed in a section 7 report include:

- the enquiries undertaken, including who was seen and where (missing appointments may be listed)
- the nature of the application which gave rise to the court-ordered enquiry
- the details of issues in dispute
- whether there is any measure of agreement between the parties
- whether there is any prospect of agreement being reached without the continued involvement of the court
- the present arrangements for the child
- the matters set out in the welfare checklist (see chapter eleven)
- the 'no-order' principle.

## Options available to the court

The report should include a reasoned assessment of the options open to the court including:

- the parties' proposals
- their likely consequences
- the wishes and feelings of the children
- referral for mediation.

A recommendation is not essential but it is preferred by most courts and should be included if you have formed a view about the appropriate course of action.

## Family assistance order

In 'exceptional circumstances' (i.e. not routinely), a court may make a family assistance order under section 16, for six months or a shorter period. This requires a CAFCASS officer or a social worker to advise, assist and (where appropriate) befriend any named person who may include:

- any parent (including the unmarried father) or guardian
- any person with whom the child is living or in whose favour a contact order is in force with respect to the child
- the child.

Before including a family assistance order in the options to be considered by the court, you must:

- identify clear plans for the work to be undertaken
- state how it can be achieved
- discuss the plan with the parties and obtain their consent
- take into account the child's wishes, although the child's consent is not required.

## Inform the parties of your conclusions

Keep the parties aware of your emerging conclusions so that the final report does not hold any surprises. Inform them that it is for the court to provide them or their representatives with a copy of your report. They should be informed when the report is submitted to the court. Unrepresented parties should be told of their right to obtain a copy of the report from the court.

## Power of the court to order an investigation

*SECTION 37*

(1) **In family proceedings in which a question arises concerning the child's welfare, where it appears to the court that it may be appropriate for a care or supervision order to be made, the court may direct the appropriate authority to undertake an investigation of the child's circumstances.**

(2) **The local authority shall consider whether they should -**

 (a) **apply for a care or supervision order with respect to the child**

 (b) **provide services or assistance for the child or his family; or**

 (c) **take any other action with respect to the child.**

(4) **The information shall be given to the court before the end of eight weeks from the date of the direction, unless the court otherwise directs.**

## Purpose of s.37 enquiry

No party may apply for a section 37 direction but parties in any family proceeding may suggest it to the court. A section 37 report should be ordered only where it appears to the court that a care or supervision order may be necessary. In an exceptional case, the court may make an interim care or supervision order[3].

Appendix G of the Protocol (see Annex Two) sets out the recommended timetable and procedure for the timely completion of report in response to a court request under section 37.

The local authority's duty to investigate is set out in section 47. Under section 37, the local authority must consider whether to apply for an order or exercise any of its other powers under the Act. These include making an offer of accommodation and applying for an emergency protection order.

## Appointment of a guardian

A guardian may be involved if an interim order has been made or if the court is considering making such an order (section 41(6)(b)).

## Planning the enquiry

In conducting a section 37 enquiry, you should:

- see the parents
- see the child unless there is enough information on which to base a decision (section 47(4))
- consider whether to consult housing, health, the police and any other local authority (who are obliged to assist you in promoting and protecting the welfare of the child).

You should follow the guidance in the Framework for the Assessment of Children in Need and their Families, DoH/ DfEE/ Home Office, TSO 2002.

## If access is refused

If refused access to the child or denied information about the child's whereabouts, the local authority should apply for an emergency protection order, child assessment order, care or supervision order unless satisfied that the child's welfare can be satisfactorily safeguarded without such an order (section 47(6)).

## If no application is appropriate

If the conclusion of your investigation is not to apply for a care or supervision order with respect to the child, a consultation with the legal adviser may not be necessary. Discuss this with your manager. The report to the court need not be very detailed. It should address:

- the work undertaken for the investigation
- the reasons for the decision not to apply for an order
- the details of any service or assistance provided, or which it is intended to provide, for the child and his family; and
- any other action taken, or which it is proposed to take, with respect to the child
- whether it would be appropriate to review the case at a later date and, if so, the date on which the review is to begin (section 37(6)).

1   16 July 1981 (Divorce: Welfare Report) [1981] 2 All ER 1056.

2   Re B (A Child) [2004] EWCH 411 (Fam), (2004) 2 FLR 142.

3   Re CE (Section 37 Direction) [1995] 1 FLR 26.

# Content and layout

Statements can be unnecessarily lengthy and sometimes it is hard to pick out the most important points. This chapter tries to help you make your statement succinct, relevant and easy to read.

## Weigh what is relevant

Incorporate in your statement only what is directly relevant to the case. Does the information in question relate to:

- one of the guiding principles of the Children Act (see chapter 1 page 4)
- the requirements of the Children Act section at issue
- a fair and balanced view
- a well-reasoned conclusion?

If the answer is 'no' to all of these questions, then the information probably need not be included.

Do not obscure the important point of your statement with unnecessary detail.

## The social worker's expertise

The court may permit opinion evidence to be given by experts.

At court, social work practitioners may give an opinion on matters for which they are suitably qualified and or experienced.

When you express an opinion, particularly in cases of suspected sexual abuse, do so within the limitations of your own expertise. If you exceed this you may be criticised by the court. Be clear about the factual basis and reasoning for any opinion you express.

## Distinguish fact and opinion

In considering which facts are relevant and any opinion which you wish to add to your evidence, you should distinguish:

- matters to be described factually as a result of your direct observations
- research carried out by others where you rely on that research to formulate your opinion
- your opinion or interpretation of behaviour or events which you have observed

- matters recorded on the file or told to you by others which are relevant to the case but which you cannot personally verify

- your opinion of the reasons for the orders being sought and the care plan based on your overall professional experience.

**Example comparing two descriptions of the same event:**

*'I made a home visit as a result of an anonymous phone call saying there was a child crying. When I got there, Mrs Callaghan let me in. Laurie was very distressed and clinging. It seemed to me that Mrs Callaghan had only recently returned and that Laurie had been left on her own. Mrs Callaghan denied this and said they had been out shopping together.'*

*The following description provides more graphic factual details as well as the basis for the social worker's opinion:*

*'Mrs Callaghan let me in. She had her coat on and there were two bags of shopping just inside the front door. Laurie was upstairs but I could hear her crying. Mrs Callaghan brought her down. Laurie was wearing a nightie which was wet and smelt of urine. She had no shoes on. Her face was puffy and blotchy and she was sobbing, gulping and hiccoughing. Laurie clung to Mrs Callaghan and would not let herself be put down or accept a bottle. I explained about the phone call. Mrs Callaghan said she had taken Laurie shopping and they had only just returned. I concluded, from Laurie's clothing and her emotional state, that the anonymous call was correct and that she had been left on her own for some time.'*

## Hearsay

Hearsay evidence relates to something not personally seen or heard by the witness. In order to remove the stress for children of giving evidence, court rules allow for hearsay evidence about what the child has said to be given by professional or lay adults[1]. The court will decide what weight, if any, to attach to hearsay evidence.

When hearsay evidence is being reported, it should be clearly identified as such together with the circumstances in which you received it. The court should be told the circumstances in which the hearsay originally came to light in order that it can make a fair judgement of the weight to be accorded to it.

In deciding the weight to attach to hearsay evidence, the court will consider:

- all the circumstances surrounding the making of the statement

- all the circumstances from which any inference can reasonably be drawn about the accuracy of the statement

- whether the statement was made at the same time that the incident occurred or was revealed

- whether the maker of the statement had any incentive to hide or misrepresent the facts

- whether the statement is corroborated by other evidence.

*Example of an account of hearsay reported by Mrs Collis, foster carer for Jeanette Ward aged five, included in the social worker's statement:*

'On 21.8.2005, while Mrs Collis was bathing Jeanette and talking about dolls, Jeanette suddenly poked her arm with her finger and said, "my mummy does this". When asked what she meant, Jeanette replied, "prick with a needle".'

*The social worker goes on to provide information to assist the court in deciding what weight to attach to the hearsay:*

'Mrs Collis report that Jeanette's remarks were spontaneous. Mrs Collis has never met Ms Ward and I know no reason why Mrs Collis would misrepresent this incident. Ms Ward acknowledges smoking cannabis but strongly denies using needles.'

*Particular care is needed to avoid presenting the conclusions of others without supporting the facts.*

**Examples of poor practice:**

'Mrs Moston has a very explosive temper. In the view of some professionals who have previously worked with her, when she is under pressure she is likely to act irrationally.'

'The police officers were shocked and dismayed at the state of the home, particularly the provisions made for the children.'

'The foster placement broke down due to what the foster carer described as wild behaviour.'

'Mrs Thomas' family have in the past expressed concern about the children's behaviour, lack of parental supervision and poor school attendance.'

The court requires factual descriptions, not unsupported opinions.

## Duty to disclose information favourable to parents

The local authority's evidence must demonstrate that the course of action it proposes is in the child's best interests. This must not be achieved by including in its statements only those facts and opinions which support the local authority's position. The court have clearly established that where the welfare of children is the paramount consideration, there is a duty on all parties to make full and frank disclosure of all matters relevant to welfare whether these are favourable or adverse to their own particular case. This includes the disclosure of information by local authorities to parents which may assist in rebutting allegations against them[2]. The statements filed by the local authority must be balanced and fair.

> **In re B [1994] 471 the mother's counsel criticised the evidence of the social worker as being selective in the material taken from the records to make up her statement. Hollings J. said 'I cannot emphasise too much that applicants such as a local authority responsible for children in their care... should not act in a one hundred per cent adversarial way... they must present [the case] in a balanced way and not fail to refer, it seems deliberately, to factors which point in a direction opposite to that which is desired by the local authority.'**

In Oxfordshire v M, the Court of Appeal upheld the view of HH Judge Harold Wilson that 'The game of adversarial litigation has no point when one is trying to deal with fragile and vulnerable people like small children. Every other consideration must come second to the need to reach the right conclusion if possible'[3]

***Example acknowledging information favourable to a parent:***

*Ms Latimer's previous child was made the subject of a care order due to non-accidental injuries and was subsequently adopted; her child Louise, aged two, is the subject of investigation for non-accidental injury.*

*While setting out reasons for concern about the recent deterioration in Ms Latimer's care of Louise, the statement nevertheless acknowledges that:*

*'An assessment of Ms Latimer's parenting skills after Louise's birth was conducted by the health visitor and social worker. They found a satisfactory standard of parenting and a warm and appropriate relationship between mother and daughter. This led to Louise's name being removed from the child protection register'.*

The principle of acknowledging favourable information also applies to giving oral evidence. You must demonstrate that you are being balanced and fair.

## Requests for disclosure to a criminal case

All requests to disclose information from social work records to criminal case must be referred immediately to the local local authority legal adviser. This applies regardless of whether the request comes from the prosecution or the defence.

## Referring to the parties

Refer to all adults as Mr, Mrs or Ms, not by their first names unless it is necessary to avoid confusion for example where there is more than one Mr X or Mrs Y. It may also be helpful to specify the relationship in the text for example, "Mrs White (the children's maternal grandmother)"

## The use of language and avoiding jargon

Your statement will be read by the parties, the court and the lawyers. Jargon ('rehabilitation', 'threshold' and 'disposal', for example) provides a form of short-hand for those with a common knowledge base, but its use is inappropriate in documents read by family members and children. Explain what you mean in simple, plain English. This will assist everyone.

Unless central to decision-making about the child, avoid inflammatory comments, particularly in the context of what one party said about the other.

Use appropriate tenses and complete sentences throughout the statement.

## Line spacing

Use a line space of at least 1$^1$/$_2$ lines or double space the lines. Your documents will be slightly longer but a great deal easier to read and absorb. Leave a blank line space between paragraphs.

Statement pages should be single-sided and numbered.

## Paragraph numbering

Numbered paragraphs make it easy to refer to specific parts of the document. Do not try to cover too much per paragraph. In general, deal with just one main point or idea and keep sentences fairly short. Where appropriate, begin a paragraph with a date. Avoids imprecise references to time such as 'during the summer' or 'at the weekend'.

## Sub-headings

Sub-headings on a separate line are useful signposts to the content of the paragraphs that follow. If a statement is particularly long (over 12 pages) it may be helpful to provide an index.

## Exhibits

Consider whether there are any documents on file which could be attached to your statement, for example:

- a contract or agreement with the family
- an assessment report
- a letter from the child or parent.

Discuss with your legal adviser how these attachments should be marked as exhibits, numbered and cross-referenced.

*Example:*

*Assessment by Pinetrees Family Centre:'This is Exhibit DN 1 referred to in the second statement of social worker Diane Nixon dated 6.6.2005'.*

## Controlling the number of updates

Since the implementation of the Children Act, most courts have experienced a significant increase in the amount of paperwork filed. It is not necessary to file a statement for every hearing. Prior to the final hearing it will be necessary to file a care plan for each child and a further updating statement will be appropriate if ordered by the court.

> **Repetition of earlier material filed by the local authority or by other witnesses or parties must be avoided. Cross-refer to other evidence filed in the proceedings where appropriate.**

You will always be given the opportunity to update information at the beginning of your oral evidence. Discuss with your legal adviser whether this is appropriate in the circumstances.

## Suggested statement contents

The local authority provides information to the court and the parties in stages, in its application and in the subsequent statements. Information is often presented in a chronological narrative but it can be more accessible to the reader if organised by key issues.

The following list at figure 5, cross-referenced to the relevant Children Act section and Handbook chapter, is not intended to be prescriptive:

Annex Three sets out a checklist for statement writing. It is not intended to be exhaustive.

---

1   *Children (Admissibility of Hearsay Evidence) Order 1993 Statutory Instrument 1993/621.*

2   *For example, Thorpe J. in Essex County Council v R [1993] 2 FLR 826; Wall J. in Re D.H. (A Minor) (Child Abuse) [1994] 1 FLR 679.*

3   *Oxfordshire County Council v M [1994] Fam 151 C.A.*

*Starting the document*
Kevin (9)

Figure 5: Selecting what should go into your statement

| Subject | Children Act section | Handbook chapter |
|---|---|---|
| facesheet | | 9 |
| the author's experience in social work and with this family | | 9 |
| list of parties, family members and others mentioned in the statement | | 9 |
| key information about court timetable | | 3 |
| background to the proceedings | 2, 10, 11 | |
| public law applications | 25, 31, 39, 43 and 44 | 6 |
| private law court ordered enquiries | 7 and 37 | 7 |
| information about the child | 1(3)(b) and (d) | 11 |
| the wishes and feelings of the child | 1(3)(a) | 11 |
| arrangements for contact | 17, 23(6) and (7) and 34 | 12 |
| working with parents and providing services | 17 | 10 |
| the parents' wishes and feelings | 22(4) and (5) | 10 |
| assessment of risk factors | 1(3)(e) | 10 |
| the capacity of the parents/carers | 1(3)(f) | 10 |
| to meet the child's present needs the care plan | | 13 |
| the conclusion, including the options available to the court and the 'no order' principle | 1(3)(g) and (5) | 14 |

# Starting the document

**9**

Effective presentation makes the content of your statement more accessible. This chapter provides of how to lay it out:

- **the face sheet**
- **the author's experience and involvement in the case**
- **the list of parties, family members and others.**

## The face sheet

On the first page, the statement should provide the following information:

- the name of the court dealing with the case
- case number (on transfer, the courts may give an additional number)
- child's name and date of birth
- type of Children Act application and relevant section
- the local authority applicant (some authorities also list the respondent parties by name)
- the name of the author, professional address and telephone number
- the date and number of the statement by this author (it may be one of a series).

## Family Proceedings Rules 1991 declaration

The document must incorporate a signed declaration that '1, ...... , social worker of ...... . declare that this statement is true and that I make it knowing it may be placed before the court in these proceedings'. This declaration normally appears at the end of the main body of the statement.

Many authorities also include a notice of the confidential status of the statement.

Appendix B of the Protocol gives guidance on Standard Documents and prescribes the contents of the initial social work statement that must be filed within 2 days of the issue of the care or supervision order application. The statement should be 'strictly limited' to the following evidence:

- The precipitating incidents(s) and background circumstances relevant to the grounds and reasons for making the application including a brief description of any referral and assessment processes that have already occurred
- Any facts and matters that are within the social worker's personal knowledge
- Any emergency steps and previous court orders that are relevant to the application
- Any decisions made by the local authority that are relevant to the application
- Information relevant to the ethnicity, language, religion, culture, gender and vulnerability of the child and other significant persons in the form of a family profile together with a

narrative description and details of the social care services that are relevant to the same

- Where the local authority is applying for an interim care order and/or proposing to remove or is seeking to continue the removal of a child under emergency protection: the local authority's initial proposals for the child including placement, contact with the parents and other significant persons and the social care services that are proposed

- The local authority's initial proposals for the further assessment of the parties during the proceedings including twin track planning

- The social work timetable, tasks and responsibilities so far as they are known.

**Example:**

---

**THIS STATEMENT IS CONFIDENTIAL AND MUST NOT BE DISCLOSED WITHOUT PERMISSION OF THE COURT**

                                             **Author**

                                             **statement No:**

                                             **Dated:**

                                             **On behalf of the applicant**

                                             **Case No:**

**In the** _____ **Family Proceedings Court**

**In the matter of** _____ **d.o.b.** _____

**Children Act s. 31 application for a care or supervision order**

**between** _____ **County Council, applicant**

**and** _____ **First respondent**

**and** _____ **Second respondent**

**and** _____ **(child's name & d.o.b.) Third respondent**

---

**Statement of Robert Whitaker, social worker**

---

**I Robert Whitaker, social worker of** _____ **CC, declare that this statement is true and that I make it knowing it may be placed before the court in these proceedings.**

**Signed** _____ **Date** _____

---

## Author's experience

The statement should begin with a summary of your qualifications and relevant experience, for example:

| BA 1985 | CQSW 1992 | |
| --- | --- | --- |
| 1988-90 | Junior school teacher | |
| 1992-94 | Social worker | Referral and Assessment Team |
| 1994-date | Social worker | Child Protection Team |

You should also describe the basis for your knowledge for example:

*'I make this statement based on my direct experience as the child's social worker since January 1994, and also on previous social work records. In describing recent events, I have drawn on information provided by WPC K. O'Neill and GP Dr M. Patel.'*

## Explain who's who and what you are seeking

It is helpful to the court to open your statement with a list of parties to the proceedings, family members and other persons to whom you intend to refer.

At the beginning of your statement you should set out succinctly what it is you are applying for, whether or not you are seeking an interim order and where the child is currently living.

Where there is more than one family grouping, a family tree or genogram is particularly useful.

Guidance on compiling a genogram can be found in Assessing Children in Need and their families; Practice Guidance, DoH, TSO 2005.

## Ethnic minority names

Ask how the individual's name should be listed and which is the personal name, which (if any) is the family name and which is used as a surname. Do not assume that everyone will have a surname in the usual British sense or a family name, or that the family name will necessarily come last[1].

**Example: Family tree**

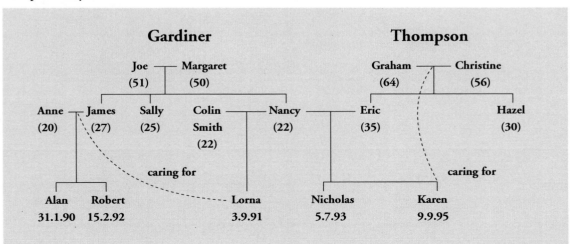

1   *Judicial Studies Board Ethnic Minorities Advisory Committee (1994) Names and Naming Systems. A summary of this paper was serialised as follows in The Magistrate:*

*Names and Naming Systems, July/August 1994 p. 111*

*Hindu Names, September 1994 p. 139*

*Sikh Names, October 1994 p. 158 and 168*

*Muslim Names, November 1994 pp. 186 and 187*

*Chinese Name, December 1994/January 1995 p.209.*

# The parents

## 10

Your statement should describe how the local authority has discharged its responsibility to:

- **work with parents**
- **provide services**
- **consider the wishes and feelings of parents and others**
- **assess risk.**

---

*SECTION 17*

The local authority has a duty to safeguard and promote the welfare of children in need in its area. As far as possible, this is best achieved by providing services appropriate to those children's needs to keep the family together.

---

## Providing services and working with parents

Albeit that in 70% of s 31 cases, children are permanently removed from their birth parents[1], care proceedings should not divert a local authority from continuing to work in partnership with parents[2]. The Children Act Advisory Committee emphasises that both the local authority and the parents have 'a role to play, often simultaneously, in the case management of a child at risk'[3].

Your evidence should describe:

- details of the services, if any, offered or provided to this family
- details of inter-agency working to support the family
- the period over which services were offered or provided
- the response of the parents and the level of take-up of the services offered
- reasons given by the parents if refusing services
- agreements made with the parents
- why the provision of services on a voluntary basis is not considered adequate to safeguard the child's welfare
- how the local authority plans to work with the parents if an order is made.

> **Section 22(4) and (5)**
>
> **Before making any decision regarding a child whom they are looking after, or proposing to look after, a local authority shall, so far as is reasonably practicable, ascertain and give due consideration to the wishes and feelings of:**
>
> • **the parents**
>
> • **anyone else with parental responsibility**
>
> • **other relevant people.**

The way in which this consultation process was carried out and the responses of the child, family and others to the local authority action should be described in the local authority's evidence.

## Assessing risk

The welfare checklist (section 1(3)) directs the court to pay particular regard to the potential risk to the child and the capacity of parents and relevant others to meet the child's needs. In assessing the child's situation and the likelihood of future harm, factors to be considered include[4]:

• evidence of previous injuries or abuse

• the risk of physical, sexual or emotional abuse or neglect

• serious personality problems or pathological patterns of behaviour

• evidence of the parents' capacity to change

• the degree of responsibility accepted by the parents for the child's situation

• the capacity of a non-abusing parent to protect the child

• whether there is someone within the family willing and able to protect the child.

You should weigh up to what extent the parents:

• recognise the need for help and will cooperate with those providing it

• show affection to the child and put the child's needs first

• are capable of sticking to agreed arrangements.

---

1  *Review of the Child Care Proceedings System in England and Wales, May 2006, www.dca.gov. uk/laid/childcare.htm*

2  *Department of Health (1991) The Children Act 1989 Guidance and Regulations Volume 3, Family Placements para. 2.19. HMSO.*

3  *Annual Report 1992/93 p. 34.*

4  *Timms J. (1995) Children's Representation - A Practitioner's Guide. Sweet and Maxwell. Pp. 166-167.*

*Explaining to the child*
Lucy (7)

# The child

## 11

This chapter discusses the welfare principle and the welfare checklist giving particular attention to the child's:

- background
- wishes and feelings

The use of centile charts is explained.

## The welfare principle - the child's welfare is paramount

*SECTION 1(1)*

Before taking any decision, the court must put the child's welfare first.

The welfare checklist

*SECTION 1(3)*

The court is directed to pay particular regard to the following factors:

- the wishes and feelings of the child concerned (considered in the light of his age and understanding)
- his physical, emotional and educational needs
- the likely effect on him of any change in his circumstances
- his age, sex, background and any characteristics of his which the court considers relevant
- any harm which he has suffered or is at risk of suffering – as a result of an amendment to the Children Act 1989 brought in by the Adoption and Children Act 2002 this definition of harm now includes 'for example, impairment suffered from seeing or hearing the ill-treatment of another' and the court is likely to regard it as equally relevant here.
- how capable each of his parents, and any other person in relation to whom the court considers the question to be relevant, is of meeting his needs
- the range of powers available to the court under the Children Act in the proceedings in question.

## Scope of the welfare checklist

Courts must consider the checklist in all applications relating to local authority care and supervision of children and in contested section 8 order applications (sections 1(4), 8(4)). In other applications, you may wish to address the welfare checklist in your statement as an aid to the court's decision making. The checklist can be a useful test of relevance in deciding what should be included in your written evidence but it is not exhaustive.

Harm is discussed in chapter six. Risk and parental capacity are dealt with in chapter ten.

## Give due consideration to the child's background

---

*SECTION 22(5)(C)*

**Before making any decision regarding a child whom they are looking after, or proposing to look after, a local authority shall, so far as is reasonably practicable, ascertain and give due consideration to the child's:**

- **racial**

- **cultural**

- **religious**

- **linguistic**

**background.**

---

Effective action to prevent discrimination requires significantly more than willingness to accept all people as equal or to invest an equal amount of time and effort in different cases. To ensure that families from a different background are not disadvantaged, the origin, nature and extent of differences in circumstances and need must be properly understood and addressed.

*'Ensuring equality of opportunity does not mean that all children are treated the same. It does mean understanding and working sensitively and knowledgeably with diversity to identify the particular issues for a child and his/her family, taking into account experiences and family context'* – Framework for the Assessment of Children in Need and their Families, TSO 2002.

Assessing Children in Need and their Families: Practice Guidance, TSO 2005, includes sections on assessing black children in need and the needs of disabled children and their families.

*Example alerting the court to concerns about language and the family's ability to communicate:*

*'During the period of the interim care orders a communication difficulty has arisen between Shamim (aged three) and his mother Mrs Khan. Shamim has forgotten his native language and his English is sometimes better than his mother's. Mrs Khan tries to speak English to Shamim and Urdu to Ali (aged eighteen months).'*

*Examples from family members interviewed by the Family Rights Group[1]:*

*'We are two totally different cultures ... They expect children to be brought up in white middle class way. We have different ways of disciplining our children, teaching them, playing with them ... We give*

*them more responsibilities in life. They are using it in the wrong way because of the differences and looking at my culture negatively and not taking into account that we are different and that my culture may be the reason for doing things in a particular way.'*

*'Social services and the court gave very little attention to our race and culture in arranging the children's care and reaching a decision. The court should have had some evidence of cultural background ... The court should make room for people who come from different cultural backgrounds.'*

***Being well informed is essential in order to make a proper assessment of what is the best interests of children. You should:***

- ask families about life-styles, child rearing and cultural patterns and expectations of service[2]

- acknowledge the importance of the family's own traditions[3]

- explain any relevant social or cultural factors which may not otherwise be understood by the court

- identify sources of advice and help so that the necessary experience and resources are available where needed.

## Give due consideration to wishes and feelings

> **SECTION 22(4) AND (5)**
>
> **Before making any decision regarding a child whom they are looking after, or proposing to look after, a local authority shall, so far as is reasonably practicable, ascertain and give due consideration to the wishes and feelings of the child (having regard to age and understanding).**

The way in which this task was approached and the response of the child to the local authority action should be described in your evidence.

> **UN Convention on the Rights of the Child Article 12**
>
> **1. States Parties shall assure to the child who is capable of forming his or her own views the right to express those views freely in all matters affecting the child, the views of the child being given due weight in accordance with the age and maturity of the child.**
>
> **2. For this purpose, the child shall in particular be provided the opportunity to be heard in any judicial and administrative proceedings affecting the child, either directly or through a representative or an appropriate body, in a manner consistent with the procedural rules of national law.**

# Referring to percentile charts

Where a child may be failing to thrive, the health visitor should be asked to put together a centile chart for the child and to document any investigations into whether the are organic reasons for concern. Is the child passing the development milestones of babyhood and childhood?

Preprinted percentile (or centile) charts provide information about the average height, weight and head circumference for a child of a given age. The data are displayed on five lines. the middle of which is the average, or 50th centile. This means that 50 per cent of children have measurements above and 50 per cent below these figures. The other lines show the 97th, 90th, 10th and third centiles.

The starting point for screening purposes is to consider children at the third and 97th centile as outside the norm. Although further investigation of children in these cut-off areas is appropriate, not all will turn out to be abnormal.

Percentile charts are used to plot the weight of an individual child over time. The pattern of growth over time is important, particularly where this departs from the norm. Once a child has reached the age of four months and has established a pattern of growth, he or she is likely to remain on the centile. If the chart shows that the child's weight, height or a baby's head circumference is falling away from the centile formerly followed, this gives rise to concerns of physical and/or emotional deprivation unless the loss is caused by organic illness. It is important to continue to chart the weight changes of children in care as 'failure to thrive' may be followed by 'catch up' growth (after placement in foster care for example) suggestive of a change in the child's well-being[4].

**The interpretation of percentile charts is the responsibility of medical professionals.**

*Making my voice heard*
Martin (13)

---

1   Lindley B. (1994) On the Receiving End: families' experiences of the court process in care and supervision proceedings under the Children Act 1989. Family Rights Group. pp. 56-57.

2   Department of Health (1991) The Children Act 1989 Guidance and Regulations Volume 3 Family Placements paras. 2.57, 2.72. HMSO.

3   Department of Health (1995) Challenge of Partnership in Child Protection: Practice Guide para. 2.60. HMSO.

4   A Child in Trust (1985) Report of the Panel of Inquiry into the circumstances surrounding the death of Jasmine Beckford. London Borough of Brent pp. 70-72.

# The local authority plan for contact

# 12

This chapter describes key issues concerning contact to be addressed in the local authority's care plan, other aspects of which are discussed in the next chapter. The Children Act emphasises the responsibility of the local authority:

- to promote the upbringing by their families of children who are in need (section 17)
- to enable children to live with their parents, relatives or friends (section 23(6))
- to place children near their home and together with their brothers and sisters (section 23(7))
- to allow reasonable contact between a child in the care of the local authority and persons for whom there is a statutory presumption of contact others with whom contact will benefit the child (section 34).

Local authority proposals are likely to be scrutinised closely at both interim and final hearings in most Children Act cases, because the Act gives the court the power to specify the nature of contact including frequency, duration and venue.

## Contract integral to the care plan

The interests of the majority of children are best served by efforts to sustain or create links with their natural family. There is a presumption that it will be in the child's interests to have contact with his or her parents. Contact should be seen as an integral part of the overall care plan for each child rather than as an issue to be decided separately.

## Clarity of purpose essential

Your witness statement must be clear about the purpose and benefit of contact for the child. This has to be assessed solely in terms of the child's interests. Contact which is working towards rehabilitation is likely to differ from contact which serves to maintain some links but is working towards permanency elsewhere.

Contacts, however occasional, may continue to have a value for the child even when there is no question of returning to the family.

Contact can keep alive for a child a sense of his origins and may keep open options for family relationships later in life[1]. 'We find balm and comfort applied to the wounds of separation when they should be kept open and salted'[2]. Where face to face contact is likely to be harmful to the child, other forms of contact should be explored.

## Presumption of contact with wide network

**Ensure that you have full information about the network of relatives and friends important to the child.**

For children looked after under a court order or in accommodation, the local authority must 'endeavour to promote contact' between children and their parents, guardians, anyone else with parental responsibility, relatives, friends and others connected with them, such as teachers, unless it is not reasonably practicable or consistent with the child's welfare[3].

Even where it proposed to terminate contact between the child and parents, there remains a general duty on the local authority to promote contact with grandparents, brothers and sisters, half brothers and sisters and other relatives. The level of intensity of the need for contact should be considered for each relationship. The question of whose welfare is paramount in this area can be complex, especially if private, public and adoption law issues intermingle. It is advisable to seek legal advice.

The presumption of contact between parent and child applies not only to care proceedings but also when the child is the subject of an emergency protection or child assessment order. Note however that the presumption of contact does not however apply when a child is made the subject of a placement order for adoption.

If the local authority is seeking to overturn the presumption of contact, it must show why the circumstances are so exceptional and why contact presents such a severe risk as to justify an order allowing the local authority permission to refuse contact between the child and their parent.

---

*SECTION 34*

- **Requires the authority to allow the child reasonable contact with his parents or guardian, or a person who, immediately prior to the making of the care order, had care of the child under a residence order or an order of the High Court.**
- **On an application made by the authority or the child, the court may make such an order as it considers appropriate with respect to the contact which is to be allowed between the child and any named person.**
- **On an application made by the authority or the child, the court may make an order authorising the authority to refuse to allow contact between the child and any named person who is mentioned in section 34(1) and named in the order.**

---

An order permitting the local authority to refuse contact does not stop contact, it merely gives the local authority the power to stop contact. If contact is stopped and then resumed the local authority should seek to discharge the section 34(4) order.

## 'Reasonable' contact is objective test of child's welfare

For children looked after under a court order, the local authority must allow reasonable contact with parents, guardians and anyone with a residence order. 'Reasonable' means 'objectively reasonable' which is not the same as contact at the local authority's discretion[4]. Case law is not clear as to whether indirect contact could be construed in certain circumstances as 'reasonable contact'. The court can order contact with a child in care if the court determines that contact is in the child's best interests even if contact was not in the local authority's long-term plans[5].

## Consultation is necessary

In order to encourage consultation and agreements about contact which all parties can accept as 'reasonable', before making a care order the court must invite the parties to comment on the local authority's proposals for contact (section 34(11)). Your plan should identify key persons in the child's life and describe what steps have been taken to consult, not merely to inform, them about proposed contact arrangements[6].

## Contact plan to inform placement decision

Where possible, arrangements for contact should be made before the child is placed. The need for contact should inform the decision about what placement would be best for the child.

## Details of the contact plan

Visits should enable parents and others to engage in normal everyday activities with their children. The plan must consider the short-term and long-term goals of contact. Issues to be address include[7].

- the child's wishes
- contact in the short- and long-term
- any agreement reached by the parties about contact or efforts to reach agreement
- frequency and length of sessions
- whether supervision is necessary and, if so, by whom
- transportation (arrangements for the child and those with whom contact is proposed)
- escort for the child while being transported
- details of the advice and support to be provided to parents to maximise the benefits of the contact to the child
- provisions for financial help to support visits[8]
- whether overnight stays are appropriate and if so, who else is likely to be in the house overnight.

# Setting

State where contact should take place and give reasons if the home of the person seeking contact is not appropriate. The court can only order contact at a specific venue if it is the property of the local authority or a willing agent.

## The purpose of supervision

If the local authority proposes that visits should be supervised, the plan should be clear about why this is necessary and give some indication of for how long supervision is contemplated. If supervision is part of an assessment of the parent-child relationship or of the ability to parent, then the plan should make clear the purpose of the assessment and provide the qualifications of the worker(s) involved.

If supervision is, alternatively, to ensure that some behaviour does not occur, the concerns need to be made clear in the contact plan. Appropriate persons to perform this supervisory task may include relatives and family friends.

## Review of contact provisions

Contact plans should specify:

- when they will be reviewed and by whom[9]
- how the parents and child will participate
- that arrangements, including supervision of sessions will be reviewed to ensure that they are not unnecessarily restrictive[10].

The monitoring of the contact plan should take into account the possibility that a particular placement may need to be changed because it is interfering with the maintenance of good contact.

## Taking account of circumstantial barriers to contact

For school-age children, contact is likely to be offered after school. For parents and other family members, evening or weekend contact may be more desirable. The plan should be as flexible as possible and take into account of problems arising from distance, lack of public transport, cost of travel and commitment to other children at home.

> **The plan should be creative in addressing ways to maintain contact between children and families. Practical support should be provided before a judgement is made as to whether parents are motivated to maintain links. Families should be told if their motivation is being tested.**

## Contact may take many forms

If your plan does not propose face-to-face meetings, alternative arrangements should be considered such as letters, cards, phone calls, text messages, video phone calls, email exchange, reasonable presents and exchange of photographs. Frequency and routeing (i.e. direct or through a named third party) should be considered. Parents are likely to require advice about what is appropriate in these circumstances.

## Restricting contact

Section 34(6) empowers a local authority to refuse to allow contact as a matter of urgency (i.e. as a result of a recent problem, not to solve long-standing difficulties) for no more than seven days. In order to extend this period it is necessary to apply for an order under section 34(4).

If you consider that the child has valid reasons for not wanting contact with someone, you should seek legal advice about whether it should be the local authority or the child who makes the application to stop contact (section 34)(4)).

Where contact is to be terminated, sensitive arrangements need to be made for farewell visits.

## Children's experience of contact visits

Children are likely to manifest distress or difficult behaviour before, during and after contact session. In describing such behaviour to the court, it is important to be objective and to take account of possible different reasons for such behaviour.

The plan should address the need to support children, families and carers to cope with upset resulting from contact so that they can continue to visit or support the visits[11].

It is important to obtain the views of the child, parents, supervisor and foster carer about contact sessions.

Even when the threshold criteria are satisfied and a care order is to be made, ongoing contact can be beneficial for instance in order to:

- Give the child the security of knowing the parents still love them
- Avoid giving the child a sense of loss or abandonment
- Allow the child to commit to the new family with the seal of approval of the birth parents
- Give the child a sense of family and identity[12]

These benefits can apply to adoption as well as permanent foster placement.

## Openness in adoption

Consider carefully whether a 'clean break' is in the best interests of the child. Adoption with contact will not automatically impede the child's bonding with the new family. Children are capable of forming new relationships and attachments without necessarily having to shed existing ones[13]. Now under the Adoption and Children Act 2002, the court must have regard to a welfare checklist including the relationships that the child already has and likelihood and value of them continuing of.

Openness can take many different forms. What is appropriate will vary according to the needs of the child and the circumstances of the adoption[14]. Where openness is in the child's best interests, the local authority must seek suitable adoptive parents with the specific needs of the child in mind[15].

Contact may be more appropriate for older children who already have a strong relationship with a relative. However, some older children may want to make a completely clean break. On the other hand, some adoptive parents of younger children may feel that it is in the child's interests to grow up having occasional contact with his or her mother. The child's wishes about contact may change significantly as he or she grows up. The child may come to feel overwhelming commitment to the adoptive family and draw back from contact, or may decide after several years to seek contact with a relative for the first time[16].

Case law on adoption with contact is technical and its continuing relevance will have to be carefully considered in light of the new adoption legislation (the Adoption and Children Act 2002) , the final parts of which were implemented in December 2005.

It is likely that a contact order, placing conditions on adopters regarding contact will only be made in exceptional circumstances[17]. Legal advice should be sought before making a recommendation since this is a highly delicate matter; if the adoptive parents are not in agreement with the plan for contact it could potentially jeopardise the placement and the long term plans for the child.

## Special Guardianship Orders

The Adoption and Children Act 2002 also introduced special guardianship orders. They provide a legal means of securing permanency for children who cannot grow up with their birth families. Unlike adoption, an order does not remove the parents' parental responsibility. You should discuss the suitability of such an order with your legal adviser if you are considering adoption. In certain circumstances, for instance for older children who do not wish to break legal ties with their birth parents, this may be a better alternative. Special guardianship orders give legal permanency and security.

---

1    Department of Health (1991) The Children Act 1989 Guidance and regulations Volume 3, Family Placements para. 6.9. HMSO.

2    Millham S., Bullock R., Hosie K., and Haak M., (1986) Lost in Care: the problems of maintaining links between children in care and their families. Gower. P. 232.

3    Children Act Schedule 2, para. 15(1).

4    Re P (Minors) (Contact with Children in Care) [1993] 2 FLR 156.

5    Re B (Minors) (Termination of Contact: Paramount Consideration) [1993] 1 FLR 543.

6    Department of Health (1995) Looking after Children Placement Plan Part Two: 5.

7    Department of Health (1995) Looking after Children Placement Plan Part One: 11-13; Placement Plan Part Two: 5.

8    Children Act Schedule 2 para 16.

9    Department of Health (1955) Looking after Children Care Plan: 19-22.

10   Department of Health (1991) *The Children Act Guidance and Regulations Volume 3, Family Placements* para. 6.38. HMSO.

11   Ryan M. (1994) *The Children Act 1989 Putting it into Practice. Chapter 7: Contact.* Arena.

12   *Re E (A Minor) (Care Order: Contact)* [1997] 1 FLR 171.

13   Wedge P. and Thorburn J. (1986) *Finding Families for 'Hard-to-Place' Children - evidence from research.* British Association for Adoption and Fostering.

14   Department of Health and Welsh Office (1992) *Review of Adoption Law - Report to Ministers of an Interdepartmental Working Group _ A Consultation Document* para 4.2.

15   *Re E (A Minor) (Contact)* 1993 Fam 671.

16   Department of Health and Welsh Office (1992) *Review of Adoption Law - Report to Ministers of an Interdepartmental Working Group _ A Consultation Document* para 5.2. and 5.3.

17   *Re C (A Minor) (Adoption Order: Conditions)* [1998] 2 FLR 159.

# The local authority plan for care of the child

# 13

When considering a local authority application, the court expects to receive a plan containing:

• clear objectives for the care of the children

• a strategy for their achievement.

There is a prescribed format for a care plan submitted in court proceedings in Appendix F (paragraph 20) of the Protocol (see Annex Two).

Plans for contact are an integral part of the care plan (see previous chapter).

## Look into the future

Unless there are clear indications that restoration to the family is not a viable option, care plans should be made with the possibility of eventual return in mind[1].

## The need for a plan

A plan must be submitted in support of an application for a section 31 care or supervision order[2]. The Protocol states that an interim care plan should be prepared, filed and served so as to be available to the court for the Case Management Conference. The local authority will also be expected to provide a final care plan later in the proceedings in advance of the final hearing. The care plan should be endorsed by a social services manager and comply with the Local Authority Circular on care plans (LAC (99) 29) in England and NAFWC 1/2000 in Wales.

The case management judge will consider the local authority planning and if necessary can make directions for 'twin track planning' to be considered. That is, more than one avenue is explored at a time for permanence for the child. Twin track planning can result in significant time savings. The court will not be sympathetic to local authority claims that it lacks the necessary resources for twin track planning.

The court has a duty to scrutinise critically the care plan to satisfy itself that it will promote the child's welfare. With the exception of contact, the court cannot compel the local authority to follow a particular plan, even where the guardian is not in agreement with the local authority view. The court's only sanction is to refuse to make a care order. The court will only do this in rare circumstances where it considers it necessary to retain control of the case by means of a series of interim care orders[3].

Where the court considers the proper outcome to be finely balanced between a care order and a supervision order, an unacceptable care plan may tip the balance in favour of a supervision order.

A properly constructed care plan is essential to enable the court to take into account all known facts when making its decision. The amount of evidence that should be presented in support of the plan will vary from case to case. Mr Justice Wall stated that it was good sense of the court and the advocates to:

*'strike a proper balance between the need to satisfy the court as to the appropriateness of the care plan and over-zealous investigation into matters properly within the local authority's administrative discretion. It should be rare for the court's dissatisfaction with the plan to be such as to prevent the making of the final care order in a case where it was satisfied both as to the threshold criteria and that a care order was in the child's best interests.*[4]

## One plan per child

A separate plan is needed for each child involved.

## Is the care plan viable?

**The care plan should:**

• **identify the child's best interests**

• **address the least detrimental alternative for the child**

• **be based on a realistic allocation of resources.**

**It may be necessary to acknowledge that a particular level of service is not available for resource reasons. Avoid describing a resource-led decision as being in the child's best interest unless it is so.**

## The overall plan

Tell the court whether the overall plan for this child includes:

• time limited assessment

• remaining with the family through provision of support services, including respite care

• return to the birth family within one month/ six months/ eventual return (indicate within how many months)

• living with relatives/ friends

• supported living in the community

• independent living

• special residential placement (e.g. hospital unit)

• long-term placement with foster carers (no return to the birth family is anticipated)

• other services to be provided by the authority or other agencies

- adoption
- special guardianship
- other (specify).

If a placement has been found, provide:

• the address (if appropriate to disclose this information)

• information about supporting the placement

• its expected duration and how long the child will need to be looked after by the local authority

• the contingency plan if the preferred placement is not available or breaks down

• arrangements for ending a voluntary placement.

## Long term-needs

What long-term needs does the child have which the placement must meet? The following issues must be considered:

- ongoing physical and mental health conditions, illnesses or disabilities
- education
- identity - the child's gender, disability, ethnic origin, language and communication, religion or culture.

## Key tasks

What needs to be done before this plan can be achieved?
Identify:

- who has overall responsibility
- the key tasks
- who is assigned to carry them out
- target dates.

What is the day-to-day role of the parent(s) in relation to the child?

If any of the child's needs cannot be met at present, Identify:

• what plans will be made to meet them in the future

• the priority needs and how they should be addressed.

The plan must consider arrangements for contact (see the previous chapter).

## Notification

The care plan should be notified in writing to the parents, the child, other carers, representatives of other agencies involved with the child and others with a sufficient interest in the child. Parents and children should be given a personal explanation of what the plan entails and the reasoning behind it, particularly if the long-term plan is a permanent placement away from the family.

## Reviewing the plan

The care plan must specify:

- the time and location of the first review
- whether the carers and parents have been given the dates and venues of all reviews and planning meetings
- the names of those with whom the plan has been discussed
- the explanation why any of those listed have not been consulted or why they disagree with any provisions of the plan
- details of the social worker and family placement worker, the frequency with which they will visit the placement and the details of the team leader/duty officer
- details of person(s) with authority to give consent to emergency and routine medical treatment including dental care; whether there is a signed parental consent to medical treatment; whether the carers have been given a copy of the statutory medical report
- consent, if given, (and any further comments) of the parents and child in relation to a request for accommodation.

## Plan for fostering

Where the plan is for foster placement and prospective carers have been identified, it may be appropriate for evidence about their suitability to be supplied by a social worker who knows them sufficiently well. The foster carers themselves need not give evidence.

## Plan for adoption

The Children Act Advisory Committee has taken the view that:

'Care plans should be as full as the facts of an individual case allow, For example, where a permanent substitute family is planned, it is helpful if a range of possible adopters are identified and there is no reason why the Adoption Panel should not have become involved so long as the child has not been directly involved e.g. in meetings or placement. The crucial distinction is between planning in advance of the court's decision (which is to be encouraged) and on the other hand pre-empting the decision of the court... Local Authorities should have these matters in mind when preparing the care plan in order to avoid unnecessary delay.' [5]

The court will expect that the plan will have gone to the 'best interests' panel for approval before the final hearing.

Where there is no readily identifiable pool of suitable adopters for the child in question, the process of searching for an appropriate family must be described. Where the plan recommends placement for adoption general evidence about the ease or difficulty of identifying a placement for that child will normally suffice. Prior consultation (at a minimum) with the principal officer of the adoption or family placement section is necessary.

## Placement Orders and Special Guardianship Orders

The Adoption and Children Act 2002 has introduced placement orders and special guardianship orders. Placement orders replace freeing orders and they authorise the local authority to place a child with prospective adopters. Special guardianship orders are an alternative to adoption in that a special guardian acquires parental responsibility and can exercise it to the exclusion of any other person with parental responsibility, but unlike adoption they do not extinguish the parental responsibility of the birth parent/s (see previous chapter). If the plan is for a placement order or a special guardianship order, the court will expect to see the best possible details as with fostering and adoption.

### Time estimates

Local authorities are often invited to estimate the time it will take to place a child for adoption. Those involved in court proceedings are likely to be unfamiliar with the sequence of steps required. Although it is impossible to forecast the total length of time needed to place an individual child, the authority should be able to give approximate times for the following stages, based on local experience:

- the completion of the child's permanence report
- submission of the child's name to the adoption panel for a decision concerning the child's best interests (Most courts take a dim view if this has not occurred before the final hearing. It is part of knowing whether or not a care plan is viable.)
- looking within the local authority for families already approved
- contact with other agencies
- identification of suitable families
- matching and approval by the adoption panel
- introductions between the child and prospective adopters.

Once a final care order has been made, the implementation the care plan for a child in care could give rise to a further court hearing. The child, if of sufficient understanding, or the parent can apply to discharge the care order or make an application regarding contact. The potential for a legal challenge of this sort underlines the importance of writing a care plan that is not only realistic but one that can actually be implemented as outlined.

---

1    *Bullock R., Little M. and Millham S. (1993) Going Home. Dartmouth Press, Aldershot.*

2    *Form C 13, question 3; Family Proceedings Courts (Children Act 1989) (Amendment) (No4) Rules 1994.*

3    *W and B; Re W (Care Pan) [2001] EWCA Civ 757.*

4    *Re J (A Minor) (Care Plan) [1994] 1 FLR 253.*

5    *Children Act Advisory Committee Annual Report 1993/1994, p. 32.*

Bobby (5)

# Coming to a conclusion

The conclusion constitutes your professional judgement and is the most important part of your submission to the court. Your conclusion must be based on accurate information set out in the body of the statement. You must have applied the appropriate principles. It will be easier to cope with cross-examination at court if you have set out clearly the facts, your reasoning and your conclusions.

This chapter contains suggestions about:

• reaching a well-reasoned conclusion

• reviewing your statement.

## Justifying your conclusions

### Make the conclusion flow from the rest of the statement

The document should make it clear to the reader how you arrived at your conclusions. Have you demonstrated the factual basis for each part of your conclusion? In assessing the risk to the child, have you explained what would need to change for the child not to suffer significant harm within the home?

Set out the options available to the court and assess each in turn. Your position on each option should be substantiated by the evidence in the body of the statement. Drawing these together is likely to assist the court in its own analysis and in drafting reasons for its decision.

### The 'no order' principle - is any order necessary?

> **SECTION 1 (5)**
>
> **When reaching its decision, the court must be sure that an order will benefit the child. If the court cannot be certain of this, it must make no order at all.**

The Children Act acknowledges that where possible, the best place for children to be brought up and cared for is within their own family. The Act aims to discourage court action where problems can be addressed by negotiation and to focus attention on those cases where a court order is necessary to secure the child's welfare.

When the local authority asks the court to make an order, its written evidence must demonstrate that the proposed care plan cannot be implemented without the benefit of court intervention.

The court has the power to make orders other than those applied for.

Even where there is parental agreement to the local authority plan, the statement should address:

- the extent of agreement
- whether the local authority feels confident that agreement will be maintained
- whether the local authority should share parental responsibility and if so, why the local authority should share parental responsibility.

## Take account of parties' views

The conclusions of other parties should be taken into account and the reasons for difference of opinion should be clearly recorded.

Based on your analysis, present a recommendation where appropriate to do so. It may not be appropriate to put forward a 'hard and fast' position at an early stage. Giving a provisional view in an early statement allows for a later change of position, where justified, and is likely to be seen as more balanced and reasonable.

## Develop your recommendation as a result of consultation

Describe the consultation process which has led to your recommendation. Key decisions should be taken in consultation with managers and others in the multi-disciplinary network and after consultation with the child and the family.

## Discuss with the guardian

At the time of submitting your final statement, you are unlikely to have received the report of the guardian. You should, however, have discussed the options available to the court with the guardian. Where you both reach different conclusions, be clear about your reasons for doing so. A difference of opinion with the guardian of itself does not require the local authority to change its position before the final hearing.

## Facilitate conciliation

Not all significant harm is caused by malicious intent.

Wherever possible, frame your proposals in a way which takes a compassionate view of the parents as work is likely to continue with them whether or not an order is made.

Consider whether your recommendation:

- is realistic and clearly explained
- is well-founded in the body of the statement
- takes account of the welfare checklist
- explains why the court should not apply the 'no order' principle.

# Reviewing your statement

## Look over the document

Always review what you have written. Get a colleague to look at it as well. As you read, consider whether your statement:

- complies with the requirements of the Protocol (both in terms of timing and content)

- is well-focused

- takes account of the guiding principles of the Children Act as appropriate (see chapter one)

- reflects the requirements of the relevant section of the Act

- is balanced and fair overall, giving credit where it is due to family members

- includes all relevant facts whether or not they support the local authority's conclusion

- verifies significant facts and justifies opinions

- avoids unnecessary repetition of material available in other court documents

- presents information with sensitivity, particularly in the context of what one party said about the other, unless central to decision-making about the child

- makes appropriate references to ethnicity, language, religion, culture, gender and vulnerability

- avoids applying your own cultural or moral values to other cultures (assumptions may be implicit in your choice of words) and is mindful of the need for equality of opportunity and is sensitive to individual differences/diversity

- takes account of changes that have occurred in the period leading up to the final hearing.

Louise (9)

# Giving evidence at court

# 15

Your written statement is likely to be regarded as your evidence in chief at court. This chapter suggests ways to:

• present evidence authoritatively

• help the court to incorporate your evidence into its decisions.

## Prepare for court

Read Annex Four. It will remind you of some key points before you give evidence.

## Refresh your memory about the details

Set aside time for:

•    a discussion of the presentation of the case with your legal representative

•    getting up to date with the other parties' views

•    reading and organising the case file (no loose papers)

•    flagging any papers to which you may wish to refer while in the witness box

•    reading your own statement

•    reading all other statements and the guardian's report.

When you give evidence in the witness box you will have what is called 'the witness bundle' in front of you. It will be a file of paginated papers which make up all the statements and reports that have been filed in the case. You may use the bundle to assist you in giving evidence by referring to documents where it helps you to explain your evidence to the court.

You should not be referring to documents that are unknown to the other parties though you may ask the courts permission to refer to your original file notes if necessary. Bring your original file notes to court but when you go up to the witness box leave them with your legal adviser. If the court gives you permission to refer to them the court staff will hand the file up to you in the witness box.

If you identify that any part of your statement is inaccurate or inconsistent, tell your legal adviser. Errors must be clarified to the court at the outset of your evidence.

## Acknowledge areas of agreement

During court proceedings, the parents' legal representatives may make a point of stressing differences between their position and that of the local authority. Consider carefully alternative interpretations put forward in the statements of other parties and try to identify areas of agreement. Where you have come to a different conclusion from the other parties, be ready to explain the reasons for your disagreement. Acknowledging points about which there is no real dispute will assist you in giving a balanced presentation.

It is usually apparent from the other parties' statements what facts are in dispute or 'at issue', but if you are in any doubt, discuss this with your legal adviser. The questions you will be asked at court are most likely to concern the facts 'at issue'. Think ahead about all relevant facts which will clarify your position.

## On the day

Present yourself professionally:

- bring your file
- dress appropriately for the formality of the proceedings
- punctuality is vital and if at all possible, arrive ahead of the scheduled start of court, as important decisions are often made in pre-court discussions.

The social worker witness is usually allowed to be present in court when not giving evidence.

## In the witness box

Where the local authority is the applicant, its legal representative presents an outline of the case and calls its witnesses first. They will be asked to give their job title and professional address. When witnesses give evidence by replying to questions from their own legal representative, this is called evidence in chief. However, it is likely that your statement will be treated as your evidence in chief to save time. In other words, you will merely be asked whether you agree with the content of your statement as it appears in the bundle of court documents. You may be invited to tell the court of anything that has happened in the case since you made your statement but you will not be expected to go through what is already in your statement in your evidence in chief.

The local authority has the burden of proving its case on the balance of probabilities, i.e. that it is more likely than not. This is a lower standard of proof than in the criminal courts, where the prosecution must prove its case beyond reasonable doubt.

You will be asked to go into the witness box and take the oath or a non-religious affirmation. As a professional witness, your overriding responsibility is to assist the court in making the best decision for the child.

Call the district judges in the Family Proceedings Court 'sir' or 'madam'. A High Court judge is called 'My Lord' or 'My Lady'. All other judges are 'Your Honour'. Do not worry if you forget what to call the judge, simply revert to a respectful 'sir' or 'madam' as and when you need to.

Three key techniques will make you seem at ease in the witness box, even if it is the first time you give evidence:

- **speak out clearly (practise using a confident, level tone of voice when you take the oath or affirm)**
- **when you speak, turn to face the district judges or judge, not the lawyer asking questions**
- **pause periodically, allowing those taking notes to catch up (watch the pen!).**

## Cross examination

In cross-examination, you are questioned by the legal representatives of all the other parties in turn. Lawyers are trained to use cross-examination to challenge the witness and put the opposing case. Expect to be questioned on the things you have written in your statement. Just because the proceedings are termed 'non-adversarial' this does not mean that the evidence will not be rigorously tested. Remember a great deal is at stake for the children and their families. Social work evidence often concerns the interpretation of past behaviour and future risk assessment. Make your oral evidence as factual as possible. The court can then assess the factual basis for your conclusions. Try to separate out the points you wish to make.

Listen very carefully to the questions. If you do not understand a question, ask for it to be explained. If you do not know the answer, say so. If the question asks for a response which is beyond your area of expertise or relates to an aspect of the case for which you have no responsibility or personal knowledge, state this clearly.

When responding to questions:

- take a balanced view - where possible, find something positive to say about the parents (such as their willingness to admit social workers conducting home visits) and acknowledge their positive feelings for the child, even if arguing that their parenting skills are not good enough
- if you are led to say something you did not really mean or which gives the wrong impression, set the record straight immediately
- do not feel obliged to change your answer, if it is accurate, simply because you are asked the same question in a different form/ repeatedly
- hold your ground where appropriate, but do not be afraid to concede a valid point made to you in cross-examination
- do not argue - it is the lawyer's job to test your evidence
- do not try to score points off the cross-examiner
- remember your role is to assist the court in reaching the correct decision
- direct your answers to the decision maker (Judge/s).

## Risk assessment

Giving a prognosis for the child's future is always difficult. Again, it is important to present your conclusions in a factual and balanced way, specifying the information on which your assessment is based.

## Refer to your statement or your case file notes

If you cannot remember an answer which is nevertheless contained in your statement, you may ask the court's permission to refer to your statement which will be contained in the court bundle of written evidence.

If you need to refer to your notes to answer a question, you may request the court's permission to refer to your own case notes in the file. You will be asked if you made the notes when the incidents were fresh in your mind. If you ask to refer to notes, the other parties' legal representatives are entitled to ask to look at them, though they may elect not to do so. Discuss whether you may wish to consult your notes with your legal adviser and manager before court.

## After court

Check that family members understand what has happened at court. Some people not in the courtroom, including children and foster carers, will be anxiously waiting to hear the outcome of the proceedings. Ensure that they are notified as soon as possible, even if it means making a phone call after office hours. Ask the local authority legal representative to give you feedback on the way you gave evidence. Use it as a valuable learning experience and to help you build confidence for next time.

## References

Witness preparation training materials, The Continuing Professional Development Department of The Inns of Court School of Law, The City Law School, City University.

Brayne H. and Martin G. (1994) Law for Social Workers. Chapter 8 - How to Behave in Court: Giving Evidence. Blackstone Press Ltd.

British Agencies for Adoption and Fostering (1992). Developing Your Court Skills. BAAF London.

Expert Testimony: Developing Witness Skills (training package with videos and printed booklets) British Psychological Society.

# Annex One Checklist for foster carers

This checklist aims to assist foster carers in planning the content of their statements prior to discussion with the local authority legal adviser.

## Experience as a foster carer

Tell the court about:

- the members of your household and ages of your children
- the number of years' experience you have as a foster carer
- the approximate number of children you have cared for
- training
- your experience of specialist fostering schemes
- relevant work experience.

## The placement

Inform the court of:

- date(s) when the child was placed with you
- where the child came from (own home, from another placement, from hospital etc.)
- the circumstances of the child's arrival and a factual description of the child (including marks, bruises or apparent illnesses)
- if the child is no longer with the you, the circumstances in which he/ she left.

## The child

Before giving your opinion about any specific concerns, try to describe factually the child's:

- eating
- sleeping
- toileting
- hygiene
- health
- speech
- play
- development
- behaviour.

Describe any aspects of the child that have changed during the placement.

Consider the impact on the child of visits from the social worker or other professionals.

## School

Have arrangements for school or transportation changed and if so, how? What has been the impact on the child of any change?

## Contact issues

'Contact' includes phone calls and letters between the child and family, not just visits. Distinguish a factual description of, for example, the child's behaviour before and after contact from your opinion about the impact of contact on the child. Describe:

- the circumstances of the child's contact with parents, brothers and sisters, other relatives and friends
- contact on significant events such as birthdays and religious holidays
- your involvement with child's family, if any.

## Children's experience of contact visits

Children are likely to manifest distress or difficult behaviour before, during and after contact sessions. In describing such behaviour to the court, it is important to be objective and to take account of possible different reasons for such behaviour.

## What the child said

When reporting what the child has said, explain the surrounding circumstances including the setting and what happened to prompt the child's comments. Were they spontaneous? Give dates if possible; explain whether you made a note of the conversation and if so, how soon after it took place. Consider what the child said in relation to:

- life at home
- court proceedings
- self-esteem
- relationships
- the future.

## Notes/Diary

If you have kept notes or a diary, keep it safe. The court may wish to see the original documents. Make sure the local authority legal adviser knows about the record that you have kept. It may contain vital evidence.

# Annex Two The Protocol

This Annex contains key parts of the Protocol. A complete copy can be found at www.hmcourts-service.gov.uk/docs/protocol-complete.pdf

# Appendix A: Case Management Checklist

## Objective

The following checklist is to be used for the First Hearing in the FPC, the Allocation Hearing in the Care Centre, Allocation Directions in the High Court and for the CMC

## Representation of the Child

1   Has CAFCASS been notified of any decision to appoint a Guardian. If so, has a Guardian been allocated or is the likely date of allocation known? ☐

2   Are there any other relevant proceedings. If so, was a Guardian appointed and has CAFCASS been informed of the nature/number of the other/previous proceedings and the identity of the Guardian? ☐

3   If a decision has been made to appoint a Guardian but no allocation has yet taken place by CAFCASS: are any directions necessary for the representation of the child including the appointment of a solicitor? ☐

4   Have the parties been notified of the names of the Guardian and of the solicitor appointed in form C46? ☐

5   Should consideration be given to the separate representation of the child? ☐

## Parties

6   Have all significant persons involved in the child's care been identified, in particular those persons who are automatically Respondents to the application. Are any directions required to ensure service upon a party? ☐

7   Has consideration been given to notifying a father without parental responsibility and informing other significant adults in the extended family of the proceedings? ☐

8    Should any other person be joined as a party to the proceedings (whether upon application or otherwise). Are any directions necessary for the service of documents. If so, which documents?

## ICO

9    Are the grounds for making an ICO agreed. Have they been recorded on form C22 or in a document approved by the Court?

10   If the grounds for making an ICO are not agreed has a date been fixed for an urgent hearing of the contested interim application or are the proceedings to be transferred to the Care Centre?

11   Have all case management directions been given to ensure that the contested interim hearing will be effective?

## Urgency, Transfer and Re-Transfer

12   Are there any features of particular urgency and if so what directions are necessary to provide for that urgency or to minimise delay e.g. lateral or upwards transfer?

13   Have any circumstances of complexity, gravity and urgency been considered and has any decision to transfer the proceedings to the Care Centre / High Court been made and notified to the parties?

14   Have the directions that are set out in the CCP and the FPCP been made upon transfer?

15   After transfer, have the circumstances of complexity, gravity and urgency that remain been re-considered and is it appropriate to transfer back to the Care Centre or FPC?

16   In relation to any question of re-transfer, has the availability of the Court been ascertained and have the parties been notified?

## Protocol Documents

17   **LA Documents on Issue of Application.** Are any directions necessary relating to the preparation, filing and service of those LA documents that are required by the protocol within 2 days of the proceedings being issued ?

18   **Case Synopsis.** Are any directions necessary to ensure that the LA or the Child's solicitor prepares, files and serves a case synopsis?

19   **The Court Bundle/Index.** Are any directions necessary to ensure that a court bundle is prepared and filed or that an index to the Court documents is prepared, filed and served? ☐

20   Have directions been given to update the court bundle/index, in particular the responsibility for, the format of and arrangements for updating (or the compilation of an application bundle) and whether updates can be provided to the Court / judge by e-mail? ☐

21   **Local Authority Case Management Documents.** Are any directions necessary to ensure that the LA case management documents are prepared, filed and served? ☐

22   **Other Party's Case Management Documents.** Are any directions necessary to ensure that the case management documents of other parties are prepared, filed and served? ☐

23   **Case Management Questionnaires.** Are any directions necessary to ensure that the parties prepare, file and serve case management questionnaires? ☐

24   **Recommended Reading List.** For any hearing where no case management questionnaire or schedule of issues will be available, are any directions necessary for the parties to provide the Court with a joint reading list? ☐

25   **Witness Non-Availability Form.** Are any directions necessary to ensure that a witness availab ility form and schedule of contact details are completed/updated? ☐

## Preliminary Directions

26   **Statements of Evidence from Each Party.** Have directions been given for the parties other than the LA to prepare, file and serve evidence in reply to the LA's initial social work statement? ☐

27   **Disclosure.** Have directions been given to ensure that all relevant documents are disclosed by the LA within 20 days of the First Hearing? ☐

28   **Allocation.** Have all allocation directions been given? ☐

29   **Standard Directions Form.** Has the SDF been completed and served? ☐

## Listing

30   **CMC.** Has a date and time been fixed for the CMC (between days 15 and 60). Is the date, time and time estimate recorded on the draft SDF? ☐

31 If a CMC is not to be listed have all case management directions been given for the Final Hearing and are they recorded on the draft SDF? ☐

32 **PHR.** Is a PHR necessary. Is the date, time and time estimate recorded on the draft SDF (not later than 2 weeks and no earlier than 8 weeks before the Final Hearing)? ☐

33 If a PHR is not necessary have all case management directions set out in the PHR checklist been considered in giving directions for the Final Hearing? ☐

34 **Final Hearing.** Has a date or hearing window been fixed for the Final Hearing (not later than in the 3 weeks commencing the 37th week after issue) and are the dates recorded on the draft SDF together with the time estimate? ☐

35 **Venue/Technology.** Have directions been given for the venue of each hearing and whether video link, telephone conferencing or electronic communication with the Court can be used? If so, have arrangements been made for the same? ☐

## Evidence

36 **Other Proceedings.** Has consideration been given to the relevance of any other/previous proceedings and as to whether the Judgment / Reasons given or evidence filed should be admitted into evidence? ☐

37 **Disclosure.** Has the Guardian read the social work files. If not when will that task be complete. Having read the files has the Guardian confirmed that either they contain no other relevant documents or that an application for specific disclosure is necessary? ☐

38 Are there any applications relating to the disclosure of documents? ☐

39 **The Child's Evidence.** Should evidence be prepared, filed and served concerning the child's wishes and feelings? ☐

40 **The Issues.** What are the issues in the case ☐

41 Are any directions necessary for the filing of further factual evidence (including clinical evidence of treatment) by any party and if so to which issue(s) is such evidence to be directed? ☐

42 Are any directions necessary for any party to respond to the LA's factual evidence and/or to the LA's proposed threshold criteria and schedule of findings of fact sought? ☐

43 **LA Core Assessment.** Has a core assessment been completed. If not, are any directions necessary for the preparation, service and filing of an assessment? ☐

44 **Additional Assessments and Expert Evidence.** In respect of every question relating to a request for expert evidence, is the request in accordance with the Experts Code of Guidance? ☐

45 What are the issues to which it is proposed expert evidence or further assessment should be directed? ☐

46 Who is to conduct the assessment or undertake the report, what is the expert's discipline, has the expert confirmed availability, what is the timetable for the report, the responsibility for instruction and the likely costs on both an hourly and global basis, what is the proposed responsibility for or apportionment of costs of jointly instructed experts as between the LA and the publicly funded parties (including whether there should be a section 38(6) direction? ☐

47 Are any consequential directions necessary (e.g. to give permission for examination or interview)? ☐

48 Are any directions necessary to provide the expert with documents/ further documents? ☐

49 Are any directions necessary for the conduct of experts meetings / discussions and the preparation, filing and service of statements of agreement and disagreement? ☐

50 **Ethnicity, Language, Religion and Culture.** Has consideration been given to the ethnicity, language, religion and culture of the child and other significant persons and are any directions necessary to ensure that evidence about the same is available to the Court? ☐

## Care Plans and Final Evidence

51 **LA.** Have directions been given for the preparation, filing and service of the final proposals of the LA and in particular its final statements of evidence and care plan? ☐

52 **Other Parties.** Have directions been given for the preparation, filing and service of the parents' and other parties responses to the LA's proposals? ☐

53 **Guardian.** Are any directions necessary for the preparation, filing and service of the Guardian's report? ☐

## Other Case Management Steps

54 **Advocates Meetings and Schedules of Issue.** Are any directions necessary to ensure that an advocates meeting takes place and that a composite Schedule of Issues is drafted?

☐

55 **Preliminary/Split Hearing.** Is a finding of fact hearing necessary and if so, what is the discrete issue of fact that is to be determined, by whom and when?

☐

56 **Family Group Conference / ADR.** Has consideration been given to whether a family group conference or alternative dispute resolution can be held and would any directions assist to facilitate the conference resolution?

☐

57 **Twin Track Planning.** Are any directions necessary to ensure that in the appropriate case twin track planning has been considered and where appropriate, directions given in relation to any concurrent freeing for adoption proceedings and for the filing and service of evidence relating to placement options and their feasibility. In particular have dates been fixed for the filing of the parallel plan and in respect of the Adoption/Fostering/ Permanent Placement Panel timetable?

☐

58 **Adoption Directions.** Are any directions necessary to ensure that the Adoption Practice Direction is complied with and in particular than any proposed (concurrent) freeing proceedings have been commenced?

☐

59 **Placement.** Are any directions necessary for the filing and service of evidence relating to placement options including extended family placements and their feasibility, information about the timetable for the assessment and planning processes and any proposed referrals to Adoption / Fostering and / or Permanence Panels?

☐

60 **Court's Timetable.** Has a timetable of all legal and social work steps been agreed and is the timetable set out in the Court order or as an approved document annexed to the order?

☐

61 **Monitoring and Compliance.** What directions are necessary to ensure that the Court's timetable and directions are monitored and complied with, in particular have directions been given for the certification of compliance upon ICO renewals and for any further directions or a return to Court in the event of significant non-compliance?

☐

62 **Change of Circumstance.** What directions are necessary to make provision for the parties to return to court in the event of a significant change of circumstance?

☐

63 **Preparation for Final Hearing.** Is any consideration necessary of the case management directions set out in the PHR checklist in particular:

- Use of interpreters?

- Special Measures for Vulnerable or intimidated witnesses?

- Children's evidence or attendance at court?

- Facilities for persons with a disability?

- Evidence or submissions by video or telephone conference or on paper or by e-mail?

- Video and audio recordings and transcripts?

# APPENDIX B: Standard Documents

**The following documents are identified in the protocol and their contents** are prescribed below

1  **Case Synopsis** shall contain such of the following information as is known in summary form for use at the Allocation Hearing and shall normally be limited to 2 sides of A4:

- The identities of the parties and other significant persons

- The applications that are before the Court

- A very brief summary of the precipitating incident(s) and background circumstances

- Any particular issue that requires a direction to be given at the Allocation Hearing (e.g. relating to a social services core assessment)

- Any intention to apply to transfer the proceedings to the High Court

- The parties interim proposals in relation to placement and contact

- The estimated length of the Allocation Hearing (to include a separate estimate relating to a contested ICO where relevant)

- A recommended reading list and a suggested reading time for the Allocation Hearing

- Advance notice of any other decisions or proceedings that may be relevant, to include: criminal prosecutions, family law proceedings, disciplinary, immigration and mental health adjudications

2  **Social Work Chronology** is a schedule containing a succinct summary of the significant dates and events in the child's life in chronological order. It is a running record i.e. it is to be updated during the proceedings. The schedule headings are:

- serial number

- date

- event-detail

- witness or document reference (where applicable)

3  **Initial Social Work Statement.** The initial social work statement filed by the LA within 2 days of the issue of an application is strictly limited to the following evidence:

- The precipitating incident(s) and background circumstances relevant to the grounds and reasons for making the application including a brief description of any referral and assessment processes that have already occurred

- Any facts and matters that are within the social worker's personal knowledge

- Any emergency steps and previous court orders that are relevant to the application

- Any decisions made by the LA that are relevant to the application

- Information relevant to the ethnicity, language, religion, culture, gender and vulnerability of the child and other significant persons in the form of a 'family profile' together with a narrative description and details of the social care services that are relevant to the same

- Where the LA is applying for an ICO and/or is proposing to remove or seeking to continue the removal of a child under emergency protection: the LA's initial proposals for the child including placement, contact with parents and other significant persons and the social care services that are proposed

- The LA's initial proposals for the further assessment of the parties during the proceedings including twin track planning

- The social work timetable, tasks and responsibilities so far as they are known.

4 **Schedule of Issues.** The composite schedule of issues produced by the advocates at the end of the advocates' meetings prior to the CMC and the PHR should be agreed so far as is possible and where not agreed should set out the differing positions as to the following:

- A summary of the issues in the case (including any diverse cultural or religious contexts)

- A summary of issues for determination at the CMC/PHR by reference to the questionnaires/checklists

- For the CMC: the timetable of legal and social work steps proposed

- The estimated length of hearing of the PHR and the Final Hearing

- For the PHR: whether the Final Hearing is ready to be heard and if not, what steps need to be taken

- The order which the Court will be invited to make at the CMC/PHR

# APPENDIX C: Code of Guidance for Expert Witnesses in Family Proceedings

## Objective

The objective of this Code of Guidance is to provide the Court with early information to enable it to determine whether it is necessary and / or practicable to ask an expert to assist the Court:

- To identify, narrow and where possible agree the issues between the parties

- To provide an opinion about a question that is not within the skill and experience of the Court

- To encourage the early identification of questions that need to be answered by an expert

- To encourage disclosure of full and frank information between the parties, the Court and any expert instructed

| Action | Party and Timing |
|---|---|
| **1 The Duties of Experts** | |
| 1.1 **Overriding Duty:** An expert in family proceedings has an overriding duty to the Court that takes precedence over any obligation to the person from whom he has received instructions or by whom he is paid. | |
| 1.2 **Particular Duties:** Among any other duties an expert may have, an expert shall have regard to the following duties: <br><br> • To assist the Court in accordance with the overriding duty <br><br> • To provide an opinion that is independent of the party or parties instructing the expert <br><br> • To confine an opinion to matters material to the issues between the parties and in relation only to questions that are within the expert's expertise (skill and experience). If a question is put which falls outside that expertise the expert must say so | |

| Action | Party and Timing | |
|---|---|---|
| • In expressing an opinion take into consideration all of the material facts including any relevant factors arising from diverse cultural or religious contexts at the time the opinion is expressed, indicating the facts, literature and any other material that the expert has relied upon in forming an opinion | | |
| • To indicate whether the opinion is provisional (or qualified, as the case may be) and the reason for the qualification, identifying what further information is required to give an opinion without qualification | | |
| • Inform those instructing the expert without delay of any change in the opinion and the reason for the change | | |
| **2**    **Preparation for the CMC**<br><br>**2.1**    **Preliminary Enquiries of the Expert:** Not later than 10 days before the CMC the solicitor for the party proposing to instruct the expert (or lead solicitor / solicitor for the child if the instruction proposed is joint) shall approach the expert with the following information:<br><br>   • The nature of the proceedings and the issues likely to require determination by the Court;<br><br>   • The questions about which the expert is to be asked to give an opinion (including any diverse cultural or religious contexts)<br><br>   • When the Court is to be asked to give permission for the instruction (if unusually permission has already been given the date and details of that permission)<br><br>   • Whether permission is asked of the Court for the instruction of another expert in the same or any related field (i.e. to give an opinion on the same or related questions)<br><br>   • The volume of reading which the expert will need to undertake<br><br>   • Whether or not (in an appropriate case) permission | Solicitor instructing the expert | 10 days before the CMC |

| Action | Party and Timing | |
|---|---|---|
| has been applied for or given for the expert to examine the child <br><br> • Whether or not (in an appropriate case) it will be necessary for the expert to conduct interviews (and if so with whom) <br><br> • The likely timetable of legal and social work steps <br><br> • When the expert's opinion is likely to be required <br><br> • Whether and if so what date has been fixed by the Court for any hearing at which the expert may be required to give evidence (in particular the Final Hearing). | | |
| **2.2** **Expert's Response:** Not later than 5 days before the CMC the solicitors intending to instruct the expert shall obtain the following information from the expert: <br><br> • That the work required is within the expert's expertise <br><br> • That the expert is available to do the relevant work within the suggested time scale <br><br> • When the expert is available to give evidence, the dates and/or times to avoid, and, where a hearing date has not been fixed, the amount of notice the expert will require to make arrangements to come to Court without undue disruption to their normal clinical routines. <br><br> • The cost, including hourly and global rates, and likely hours to be spent, of attending at experts / professionals meetings, attending court and writing the report (to include any examinations and interviews). | **Solicitor instructing the expert** | **5 days before the CMC** |
| **2.3** **Case Management Questionnaire:** <br> **Any party** who proposes to ask the Court for permission to instruct an expert shall not later than 2 days before the CMC (or any hearing at which the application is to be made) file and serve a case management questionnaire setting out the proposal to instruct the expert in the following detail: <br><br> • The name, discipline, qualifications and expertise of | **The Party proposing to instruct the expert** | **not later than 2 days before the CMC** |

| Action | Party and Timing | |
|--------|-----------------|---|
| the expert (by way of C.V. where possible) | | |
| • The expert's availability to undertake the work | | |
| • The relevance of the expert evidence sought to be adduced to the issues in the proceedings and the specific questions upon which it is proposed the expert should give an opinion (including the relevance of any diverse cultural or religious contexts) | | |
| • The timetable for the report | | |
| • The responsibility for instruction | | |
| • Whether or not the expert evidence can properly be obtained by the joint instruction of the expert by two or more of the parties. | | |
| • Whether the expert evidence can properly be obtained by only one party (e.g. on behalf of the child) | | |
| • Whether it is necessary for more than one expert in the same discipline to be instructed by more than one party | | |
| • Why the expert evidence proposed cannot be given by social services undertaking a core assessment or by the Guardian in accordance with their different statutory duties | | |
| • The likely cost of the report on both an hourly and global basis. | | |
| • The proposed apportionment of costs of jointly instructed experts as between the Local Authority and the publicly funded parties. | | |
| **2.4  Draft Order for the CMC:** <br> Any party proposing to instruct an expert shall in the draft order submitted at the CMC request the Court to give directions (among any others) as to the following: <br><br> • The party who is to be responsible for drafting the letter of instruction and providing the documents to the expert <br><br> • The issues identified by the Court and the questions about which the expert is to give an opinion | **Any Party** | **not later than 2 days before the CMC** |

| Action | Party and Timing | |
|---|---|---|
| • The timetable within which the report is to be prepared, filed and served | | |
| • The disclosure of the report to the parties and to any other expert | | |
| • The conduct of an experts' discussion | | |
| • The preparation of a statement of agreement and disagreement by the experts following an experts discussion | | |
| • The attendance of the expert at the Final Hearing unless agreement is reached at or before the PHR about the opinions given by the expert. | | |

**3**     **Letter of Instruction**

Solicitor instructing the expert    **within 5 days of the CMC**

3.1    **The solicitor instructing the expert** shall within 5 days of the CMC prepare (agree with the other parties where appropriate) file and serve a letter of instruction to the expert which shall:

- Set out the context in which the expert's opinion is sought (including any diverse ethnic, cultural, religious or linguistic contexts)

- Define carefully the specific questions the expert is required to answer ensuring

  - **that they are within the ambit of the expert's area of expertise and**

  - **that they do not contain unnecessary or irrelevant detail**

  - **that the questions addressed to the expert are kept to a manageable number and are clear, focused and direct**

  - **that the questions reflect what the expert has been requested to do by the Court**

- List the documentation provided or provide for the expert an indexed and paginated bundle which shall include:

  - **a copy of the order (or those parts of the order) which gives permission for the instruction of the expert immediately the order becomes available**

| Action | Party and Timing | |
|---|---|---|
| • **an agreed list of essential reading** | | |
| • **all new documentation when it is filed and regular updates to the list of documents provided or to the index to the paginated bundle** | | |
| • **a copy of this code of guidance and of the protocol** | | |
| • Identify the relevant lay and professional people concerned with the proceedings (e.g. the treating clinicians) and inform the expert of his/her right to talk to the other professionals provided an accurate record is made of the discussion | | |
| • Identify any other expert instructed in the proceedings and advise the expert of his/her right to talk to the other experts provided an accurate record is made of the discussion | | |
| • Define the contractual basis upon which the expert is retained and in particular the funding mechanism including how much the expert will be paid (an hourly rate and overall estimate should already have been obtained) when the expert will be paid, and what limitation there might be on the amount the expert can charge for the work which he/she will have to do. There should also be a brief explanation of the 'detailed assessment process' in cases proceeding in the Care Centre or the High Court which are not subject to a high cost case contract | | |
| • In default of agreement the format of the letter of instruction shall be determined by the Court, which may determine the issue upon written application with representations from each party. | | |
| **4    The Expert's Report**<br><br>**4.1    Content of the Report:**<br>The expert's report shall be addressed to the Court and shall:<br><br>• Give details of the expert's qualifications and experience | **The Expert** | **In accordance with the Court's timtable** |

| Action | Party and Timing | |
|---|---|---|
| • Contain a statement setting out the substance of all material instructions (whether written or oral) summarising the facts stated and instructions given to the expert which are material to the conclusions and opinions expressed in the report<br><br>• Give details of any literature or other research material upon which the expert has relied in giving an opinion<br><br>• State who carried out any test, examination or interview which the expert has used for the report and whether or not the test, examination or interview has been carried out under the expert's supervision.<br><br>• Give details of the qualifications of any person who carried out the test, examination or interview<br><br>• Where there is a range of opinion on the question to be answered by the expert:<br><br>  • **summarise the range of opinion and**<br><br>  • **give reasons for the opinion expressed**<br><br>• Contain a summary of the expert's conclusions and opinions<br><br>• Contain a statement that the expert understands his duty to the Court and has complied with that duty<br><br>• Where appropriate be verified by a statement of truth. | | |
| **4.2 Supplementary Questions:**<br>Any party wishing to ask supplementary questions of an expert for the purpose of clarifying the expert's report must put those questions in writing to the parties not later than 5 days after receipt of the report. Only those questions that are agreed by the parties or in default of agreement approved by the Court may be put to the expert The Court may determine the issue upon written application with representations from each party. | **Any Party** | **within 5 days of the receipt of the report** |

| | Action | Party and Timing | |
|---|---|---|---|
| **5** | **Experts Discussion (Meeting)** | The Court | at the CMC |
| 5.1 | **Purpose:**<br>The Court will give directions for the experts to meet or communicate:<br><br>• To identify and narrow the issues in the case.<br><br>• To reach agreement on the expert questions<br><br>• To identify the reasons for disagreement on any expert question and to identify what if any action needs to be taken to resolve any outstanding disagreement/question<br><br>• To obtain elucidation or amplification of relevant evidence in order to assist the Court to determine the issues<br><br>• To limit, wherever possible, the need for experts to attend Court to give oral evidence. | | |
| 5.2 | **The Arrangements for a Discussion/Meeting: In accordance with the directions given by the Court at the CMC,** the solicitor for the child or such other professional who is given the responsibility by the Court shall make arrangements for there to be a discussion between the experts within 10 days of the filing of the experts reports. The following matters should be considered:<br><br>• Where permission has been given for the instruction of experts from different disciplines a global discussion may be held relating to those questions that concern all or most of them.<br><br>• Separate discussions may have to be held among experts from the same or related disciplines but care should be taken to ensure that the discussions complement each other so that related questions are discussed by all relevant experts<br><br>• 7 days prior to a discussion or meeting the solicitor for the child or other nominated professional should formulate an agenda to include a list of the questions for consideration. This may usefully take the form of a list of questions to be circulated | Child's Solicitor | **within 10 days of the filing od the experts reports** |

| Action | Party and Timing | |
|---|---|---|
| among the other parties in advance. The agenda should comprise all questions that each party wishes the experts to consider. The agenda and list of questions should be sent to each of the experts not later than 2 days before the discussion | | |
| • The discussion should usually be chaired by the child's solicitor or in exceptional cases where the parties have applied to the Court at the CMC, by an independent professional identified by the parties or the Court. In complex medical cases it may be necessary for the discussion to be jointly chaired by an expert. A minute must be taken of the questions answered by the experts, and a Statement of Agreement and Disagreement must be prepared which should be agreed and signed by each of the experts who participated in the discussion. The statement should be served and filed not later than 5 days after the discussion has taken place | | |
| • Consideration should be given in each case to whether some or all of the experts participate by telephone conference or video link to ensure that minimum disruption is caused to clinical schedules. | | |
| **5.3 Positions of the Parties:**<br>Where any party refuses to be bound by an agreement that has been reached at an experts' discussion that party must inform the Court at or before the PHR of the reasons for refusing to accept the agreement. | **Any Party** | **at the PHR** |
| **5.4 Professionals Meetings:**<br>In proceedings where the Court gives a direction that a professionals meeting shall take place between the Local Authority and any relevant named professionals for the purpose of providing assistance to the Local Authority in the formulation of plans and proposals for the child, the meeting shall be arranged, chaired and minuted in accordance with directions given by the Court. | | |

| Action | Party and Timing | |
|---|---|---|
| **6 Arranging for the Expert to attend Court** | **Every Party responsible for the instruction of an expert** | **by the PHR** |
| **6.1 Preparation:** The party who is responsible for the instruction of an expert witness shall ensure: <ul><li>That a date and time is fixed for the Court to hear the expert's evidence that is if possible convenient to the expert and that the fixture is made substantially in advance of the Final Hearing and no later than at the PHR (i.e. no later than 2 weeks before the Final Hearing)</li><li>That if the expert's oral evidence is not required the expert is notified as soon as possible</li><li>That the witness template accurately indicates how long the expert is likely to be giving evidence, in order to avoid the inconvenience of the expert being delayed at Court.</li></ul> | | |
| **6.2 All parties shall ensure:** <ul><li>That where expert witnesses are to be called the advocates attending the PHR have identified at the advocates meeting the issues which the experts are to address</li><li>That wherever possible a logical sequence to the evidence is arranged with experts of the same discipline giving evidence on the same day(s)</li><li>That at the PHR the Court is informed of any circumstance where all experts agree but a party nevertheless does not accept the agreed opinion so that directions can be given for the proper consideration of the experts' evidence and the parties reasons for not accepting the same</li><li>That in the exceptional case the Court is informed of the need for a witness summons.</li></ul> | **All Parties** | **at the PHR** |

| Action | Party and Timing | |
|---|---|---|

## 7  Post Hearing Action

7.1  Within 10 days of the Final Hearing the solicitor instructing the expert should provide feedback to the expert by way of a letter informing the expert of the outcome of the case, and the use made by the Court of the expert's opinion. Where the Court directs that a copy of the transcript can be sent to the expert, the solicitor instructing the expert should obtain the transcript within 10 days of the Final Hearing.

**Solicitor instructing the expert** — **within 10 days of the Final Hearing**

# APPENDIX F: Social Services Assessment and Care Planning Aide-Memoire

## Days

**The reference in this appendix to "DAYS" is independent of the "DAYS" referred to in The 6 Steps**

| | Recommended Guidance | | Recommended timetable |
|---|---|---|---|
| 1 | **Referral** A referral to a Council with Social Services Responsibilities (CSSR) in England and a Local Authority in Wales (i.e. a request for services including child protection) triggers the following Government guidance: | | **On DAY 1** |
| 2 | **Initial Decision** Within 1 working day of a referral social services should make a decision about what response is required including a decision to take no action or to undertake an initial assessment. The parents or carers (the family), where appropriate, the child and (unless inappropriate) the referrer should be informed of the initial decision and its reasons by social services | | **On DAY 2** |
| 3 | **Initial Assessment** An initial assessment (if undertaken) should be completed by social services within a maximum of 7 working days of the date of the referral (i.e. 6 working days from the date of the decision about how to respond to a referral) | | **By DAY 7** |
| 4 | As part of an initial assessment social services should:<br>• Obtain and collate information and reports from other agencies<br>• Interview family members and the child<br>• In any event, see the child | | |
| 5 | At the conclusion of an initial assessment social services will make a decision about whether the child is a child in need and about further action including whether to | | |

| Recommended Guidance | Recommended timetable | |
|---|---|---|
| undertake a core assessment. It will inform the family, the child and other relevant agencies of the decision and its reasons. Social services will record the response of each person and agency consulted | | |
| 6 **Initial Assessment Record** Social services will make and keep a record of the initial assessment and decision making process. The Department of Health (DH) and Welsh Assembly Government (WAG) publish an 'Initial Assessment Record' for this purpose. | | |
| 7 **Child in Need Plan** Where social services decide that the child is a child in need they will make a plan which sets out the services to be provided to meet the child's needs. | | |
| 8 **Strategy Discussion/Record** Where social services has evidence that the child is suspected to be suffering or is likely to suffer significant harm it should ensure that an inter agency strategy discussion takes place to decide whether to initiate an enquiry under section 47 of the Children Act. This should also result in the child in need plan being updated. A record of the strategy discussion will be made. | | |
| 9 **Achieving Best Evidence in Criminal Proceedings** Where a child is the victim of or witness to a suspected crime the strategy discussion shall include a discussion about how any interviews are to be conducted with the child. These may be as part of a police investigation and /or a section 47 enquiry initiated by social services, These interviews should be undertaken in accordance with Government guidance 'Achieving Best Evidence in Criminal Proceedings'. | | |
| 10 **Complex Child Abuse Investigations** Where a complex child abuse investigation has been initiated by social services or the police there will be inter agency strategy discussions to make recommendations relating to the planning, co-ordination and management of the investigation and assessment processes in accordance | | |

| Recommended Guidance | | Recommended timetable |
|---|---|---|
| | with the guidance given in 'Working Together', 'Complex Child Abuse Investigations: Inter Agency Issues' (England only – to be published in Wales, Summer 2003) | |
| 11 | **Section 47 Enquiries** If during a strategy discussion it is decided that there is reasonable cause to suspect that the child is suffering or is likely to suffer significant harm, section 47 enquiries will be initiated by social services. This means that a core assessment will be commenced under section 47 of the Children Act 1989. It should be completed within 35 working days of the completion of the initial assessment or the strategy discussion at which it was decided to initiate section 47 enquiries. | **By DAY 42 or within 35 days of the last strategy discussion** |
| 12 | **Core Assessment** Where social services decides to undertake a core assessment it should be completed within 35 working days of the initial assessment or the date of the subsequent strategy discussion A timescale for completion of specialist assessments should be agreed with social services | **By DAY 42 or within 15 days of the last strategy discussion** |
| 13 | At the conclusion of a core assessment social services should consult with the family, the child and all relevant agencies before making decisions about the plan for the child. Social Services will record the response of each person and agency consulted. | |
| 14 | **Core Assessment Record** Social services will make and keep a record of the core assessment and decision making process. The DH and WAG publish a 'Core Assessment Record' for this purpose. | |
| 15 | **Child Protection Conferences** Where social services undertakes section 47 enquiries and it is concluded that a child is at continuing risk of suffering or is likely to suffer significant harm, social services will consider whether to convene a child protection conference. A child protection conference determines whether the child is at continuing risk of significant harm | **By DAY 22 or within 15 days of the end of the last strategy discussion** |

| Recommended Guidance | Recommended timetable |
|---|---|
| and therefore requires a child protection plan to be put in place when determining whether to place the child's name on the child protection register. It agrees an outline child protection plan. An initial child protection conference should take place within 15 working days of the last strategy discussion (i.e. by day 22) in accordance with the Government guidance given in 'Working Together to Safeguard Children: a guide to inter-agency working to safeguard and promote the welfare of children' | |
| **16**   **Decision to Apply for a Care Order** At the conclusion of the core assessment which may have been undertaken under section 47 of the Children Act and where no earlier decision has been made social services should decide whether to apply for a statutory order and should be able to identify by reference to the conclusions in the core assessment<br><br>• The needs of the child (including for protection),<br><br>• The services that will be provided,<br><br>• The role of other professionals and agencies,<br><br>• Whether additional specialist assessments are to be undertaken,<br><br>• The timetable and<br><br>• The responsibilities of those involved. | |
| **17**   **Plans** At the conclusion of a core assessment social services will prepare one or more of the following plans:<br><br>• A children in need plan<br><br>• A child protection plan for a child whose name is on the child protection register<br><br>• A care plan (where the child is a looked after child)<br><br>The DH and WAG publish formats and / or guidance for each of these plans. | |
| **18**   **Interim Care Plans** Where social services decide to make an application to the Court it will be necessary | |

| Recommended Guidance | Recommended timetable |
|---|---|
| to satisfy the Court that an order would be better for the child than making no order at all. An interim care plan should be prepared, filed and served so as to be available to the Court for the CMC in accordance with steps 3.4 and 4.1 of the protocol. | |
| **19** In cases where no core assessment has been undertaken (e.g. because the interim care order had to be taken quickly before one could be begun/completed) it should be begun/completed as soon as possible. The interim care plan should be developed from the initial assessment information | |
| **20** **Care Plans** Care Plans should be written so as to comply with the Government guidance given in LAC(99) 29 in England and Care Plans and Care Proceedings under the CA 1989 NAFWC 1/2000 in Wales. While interim care plans will necessarily be in outline and contain less comprehensive information, the plan should include details of the following:<br><br>• The aim of the plan and a summary of the social work timetable<br><br>• A summary of the child's needs and how these are to be met including<br><br>• placement<br><br>• contact with family and other significant persons<br><br>• education, healthcare and social care services<br><br>• the role of parents and other significant persons<br><br>• the views of others<br><br>• Implementation and management of the plan | |
| **21** **Emergency Protection** Where at any time there is reasonable cause to believe that a child is suffering or is likely to suffer significant harm, an application for a child assessment order or an emergency protection order may be made (among others) by social services. The child may be removed or remain in a safe place under police powers of protection. In each case agency and/or court records of the application and reasons will exist. | |

| Recommended Guidance | Recommended timetable |
|---|---|
| 22 **Adoption** Government guidance is given on the assessment and decision making process relating to adoption in England in **LAC (2001) 33** which from the 1st April 2003 incorporates the 'National Adoption Standards for England'. The processes and timescales of assessment and decision making for a child for whom adoption is identified as an option are set out in detail in the Standards. | **On DAY 1** |

# APPENDIX G: Section 37 Request

| Objective | Target time: |
|---|---|
| To provide a recommended procedure within the existing rules for the timely determination of section 37 requests by the Court | by DAY 40 |

| | Action | Party and Timing | |
|---|---|---|---|
| 1 | **The Test** Where, in any family proceedings in which a question arises with respect to the welfare of any child, it appears to the Court that it may be appropriate for a care or supervision order to be made with respect to the child, the Court may direct the appropriate local authority (LA) to undertake an investigation of the child's circumstances. | Court | on DAY 1 |
| 2 | **The Court's Request** On the same day the **Court** shall:<br><br>• Identify the LA that is to prepare the s 37 report<br><br>• Fix the date for the next hearing<br><br>• Specify the date for the s 37 report to be filed by the LA<br><br>• Direct the court officer to give notice of the order and the form C40 to the LA court liaison manager / lawyer (as set out in the CCP) by fax on the day the order is made<br><br>• Direct each party to serve upon the LA all further documents filed with the Court. | Court | on DAY 1 |
| 3 | Where a s 37 report is required in less than 8 weeks, the **Court** should make direct enquiries of the Court liaison manager / lawyer of the LA to agree the period within which a report can be written. | Court | on DAY 1 |
| 4 | Within 24 hours of the order being made (on **DAY 2**) the **court officer** shall serve on the LA a sealed copy of the order and such other documents as the Court has directed. | Court Officer | on DAY 1 |

| | Action | Party and Timing | |
|---|---|---|---|
| 5 | **LA Responsibility** Within 24 hours of the receipt of the sealed order (on **DAY 3**) the Court liaison manager / lawyer of the **LA** shall ensure that the request is allocated to a social services team manager who shall: <br><br> • Be responsible for the preparation of the report and the allocation of a social worker/team to carry out any appropriate assessment <br><br> • Ensure that the request is treated and recorded as a formal referral by social services in respect of each child named in the order <br><br> • Notify the Court and the lawyers acting for all parties of his / her identity and contact details and the identity of the team that has been allocated <br><br> • Follow Government guidance in relation to referral and assessment processes (see appendix F). | **LA** | **on DAY 3** |
| 6 | Any **assessment** including a core assessment that is undertaken by social services should be completed within 35 days of the allocation above i.e. within 36 days of the service of the sealed court order. | **Social Services** | **by DAY 38** |
| 7 | At the conclusion of the social services enquiries **social services** shall: <br><br> • Consult with the family, the child and all relevant agencies before making decisions about a plan for the child. The LA will record the response of each person and agency consulted <br><br> • Decide whether to apply to the Court for a statutory order <br><br> • File the section 37 report with the Court and serve it upon the parties on or before the date specified in the Court's order. | **Social Services** | **between DAYS 38 and 40** |
| 8 | Where social services decide not to apply for a care or supervision order they should as part of their report set out the decisions they have made and the reasons for those decisions and any plan they have made for the child (including the services to be provided) in accordance with Government guidance (see appendix F). | | |

# Annex Three Checklist for statement writing

Before you start writing you will need to know:

- The parties
- The name of the court where the case is the case being heard
- The deadline for filing the statement
- Whether the court has said what the statement is to cover
- When the legal department wants the draft statement by
- Whether you are responding to other evidence already filed
- Whether you are supplementing other evidence e.g. a previous statement
- The outcome the local authority is seeking at the hearing/ in the case
- Whether a care plan/s is also required to be filed
- What the broad outline structure of the statement looks like
- The issues or questions you need to address

You will also need access to:

- The file
- Other relevant documentary evidence not on the file
- The chronology
- Previous court documents, if there are any
- Legal advice about the relevant law
- Relevant parts of (see Annex Two) the Protocol

When it is written, ensure that your statement has:

- The court name
- The case name and number
- The author's name and statement of truth
- Page numbers
- Paragraph numbers
- Headings and sub headings
- An introduction (beginning)
- Sources of information clearly set out
- A main body (middle)
- A conclusion (end)

- Opinions, if appropriate
- Reasoning for those opinions
- One and a half or double spaced lines
- Wide margins
- Single-sided printing
- Been drafted in the first person
- No jargon
- Short, clear sentences
- Short paragraphs
- Been proof read
- No errors
- Signature and a date
- Appendices where helpful

# Annex Four Tips for Giving Evidence

(i)      PREPARE thoroughly – re read your statements and the evidence in the case

(ii)     THINK about the sort of questions you will be asked in cross-examination

(iii)    ARRIVE at court in good time and know when and where to meet your legal advisers

(iv)     DRESS smartly

(v)      WALK calmly up to the witness box

(vi)     SWEAR/AFFIRM, reading the words carefully off the card presented by the usher

(vii)    BE READY to explain your qualifications and experience

(viii)   LOOK at the questioner when you are being asked something

(ix)     LOOK at the decision maker/s when answering

(x)      TELL the court if you did not hear/understand the question

(xi)     SAY if you do not know the answer

(xii)    SPEAK slowly and clearly

(xiii)   WATCH the pen

(xiv)    USE the bundle – refer to your statement and other documents in the bundle if it helps you explain

(xv)     AVOID jargon – explain things in plain English

(xvi)    REFER to the adults as Mr/Miss/Mrs etc – not by their first names unless to avoid confusion

(xvii)   TURN OFF your mobile phone

(xviii)  PROJECT your voice so that everyone in the courtroom can hear you

(xix)    REMAIN calm and polite at all times  – you are a professional and you are not on trial nor are you there to argue with cross-examiner

(xx)     HELP the court make its decision

(xxi)    BE BALANCED AND FAIR

(xxii)   ANSWER the questions, you are not there to avoid them, and above all

(xxiii)  TELL THE TRUTH

# Annex Five Useful Web addresses in alphabetical order

www.cafcass.gov.uk

www.city.ac.uk/law

www.courtservice.gov.uk

www.dfes.gov.uk

www.everychildmatters.gov.uk

www.hmcourts-service.gov.uk/docs/protocol-complete.pdf

www.probation.homeoffice.gov.uk

www.nacro.org.uk

www.tso.co.uk

www.victoria-climbie-inquiry.org.uk/finreport/finreport.htm

# Annex Six The Human Rights Act 1998

The Human Rights Act 1998 sets out a number of rights that are enforceable in the English courts. The rights come from the European Convention on Human Rights, 1950. The Human Rights Act aims to ensure that everyone's rights are respected – this often means balancing one person's rights against another's or one person's rights against the community's as a whole.

The two articles that are usually most relevant to Children Act proceedings are Article 6 – Right to a fair trial and Article 8 – Right to respect for private and family life.

Public bodies (and this includes local authorities) can be sued if they breach a person's human rights. But you should also be aware that not all rights are absolute. For example the removal of a child under an emergency protection order will not amount to an unlawful interference with the family's Article 8 rights so long as it was a lawful and proportionate response. A "proportionate" response is one that is not excessive and is justified in the circumstances.

To be fair, balanced and proportionate, should be your aim in all cases.